There Are
No Secrets

There Are No Secrets

Professor Cheng Man Ch'ing and his Tai Chi Chuan

Wolfe Lowenthal

North Atlantic Books
Berkeley, California

ISBN 1–55643–112–0

Published by
North Atlantic Books
P.O. Box 12327
Berkeley, California 94712

Photographs by Kenneth Van Sickle
Cover and book design by Paula Morrison
Typeset by Classic Typography

Printed in the United States of America

**There Are No Secrets: Professor Cheng Man Ch'ing and his
Tai Chi Chuan** is sponsored by the Society for the Study of Native
Arts and Sciences, a nonprofit educational corporation whose goals
are to develop an educational and crosscultural perspective link-
ing various scientific, social, and artistic fields; to nurture a holis-
tic view of arts, sciences, humanities, and healing; and to publish
and distribute literature on the relationship of mind, body, and
nature.

For Tam

Acknowledgements

I want to thank Julianna Cheng, Liu Hsi-hung, Bob Smith, John Lang, Ben Lo, Nicole Gregory, Ken Van Sickle, Lin Farley, Ed Young and John Wolfe. Without their help and support this book would not have been possible.

W. L.

Preface

When Cheng Man-ch'ing died fifteen years ago I wrote that this masterless man's passing left "not only nobody equal, but nobody even second to him in Taichi" (borrowing William Haylitt's 1819 words on the death of famed handballer John Cavanagh). From what has occurred since, I'd say my words were understated. Oh yes, we have 10,000 bustling little masters whirling hither and yon, birds who, disavowing learning, pretend to know everything but understand nothing (obviously, there are still excellent teachers around but they seem overwhelmed by the number of commercial operators more in tune with the dollar than with the art.)

Taichi is now evolving into a sport of tawdry tournaments and trophies in which an internal form of moving meditation is judged by the criteria of external dance. At a recent tournament one hirsute hero frenetically did a form that was more a temper tantrum than Taichi. A chap fairly fluent in the form was flunked at the same tournament because "You looked like you were doing it at home." The judges (when asked how long she'd practiced Taichi, one judge responded, "Oh, I don't know Taichi, I'm a judge") rewarded competitive picturesque performance whereas real Taichi always smacks of hearth and home. Deep down, commercial Taichi is essentially shallow.

Likewise, push hands has been lowered to the level of junior varsity competition where it was traditionally meant to be a quiet way of testing one's form with another person while adhering to the basic principle established centuries ago of "No resistance and no letting go." Taichi derives directly from Taoism which is against all competition. Push hands–because the words we use affect our actions, in my teaching I prefer "sensing hands"–done for ego, dollars, and crowds becomes shoving hands, principles are forsaken, and Taichi goes to the demnition bow-wows (not too long ago two female teams got so excited in their win-at-all-costs Taichi that a general fist fight ensued). A young sumo wrestler would have an easy time at such tournaments.

What would Cheng Man-ch'ing have thought about this deterioration? (After all, he was more Confucian than Taoist, not against all competition, and had once introduced me to the assembled club in New York City as a man who had travelled the Orient challenging other boxers.) But I can still see him shaking his head and wagging his finger at me admonishingly and saying, after I had disposed of some worthy too energetically, "Don't use force (li), relax, invest in loss, don't be greedy." So I know what he would say. To him, if Taichi didn't accord with Shakespeare's "Use all gently" it wasn't Taichi. If it wasn't quiet and its growth achieved only gradually, it was something else. To him Taichi was, like truth, unaffected by time and fashion. One either tried to do it correctly or got away from it. The old Zen saying rampages, "If the wrong man uses the right means [Taichi], the right means work in the wrong way." Amen.

Wolfe Lowenthal's quiet little memoir will with window-opening wisdom reinforce, I think, my view of how Cheng stood on Taichi. It tells how a young writer reacted to this strange Chinese man when he appeared in New York City in the mid-1960s and stayed there for a decade before returning to Taiwan to die in 1975. In a nickel town where neurosis is a cardinal virtue, the Taichi center established by Cheng soon became an oasis of learning. In my visits there I was invariably approached by a quiet fellow with a ready smile and loads of questions. His form and sensing hands improved but he never lost his kindly ways. This led me once to tell the three seniors that the one person in the club who best exemplified Taichi was this junior. That man who has since become a teacher of the art is the author of this book.

As I read his words I had mixed emotions. Since writing about Cheng in *Chinese Boxing: Masters and Methods* (1980), much new data on him has come to hand, material I planned to use later in a new book on Taichi. I had the selfish thought that now I had been preempted. This ego-serving thought soon passed as I reflected that truth is too good to hold—it is better to have it out lest it never see daylight. Also, I saw how charmingly Wolfe had showcased Professor's words and acts and worked them into the fabric of his book. And, there was a good deal here that I was meeting for the first time. For example, I hadn't known that Cheng had had a brief fling at bowling and the image of him—brush haircut, whiskers, and robe—throwing the ball down the alley fascinated me as did the later stories of how poor Cheng was at poker and in comprehending space travel.

Lowenthal is felicitous on sensing hands, particularly on the frustration of pushing someone without moving one's own arms. With Cheng one time, he gets over-zealous and they crack heads. This made me recall a time when I pushed with Cheng and deliberately emptied my mind of intent on the chance he was reading my mind. I attacked and was shocked to feel him "against" me. He paused, laughed, and then asked, "Why did you stop? You had the advantage!" I stammered that I had been so astounded to feel him for the first time against me, that I couldn't move. We tried again and I reverted to my usual "tactical" mind and was neutralized and pushed several times for my pains. Then I erased the tactical by thinking of baseball and when I attacked, he again was against me.

But still I failed to follow up my advantage and he laughed as though he thought that I had stopped because I was wary of a trap. But it wasn't that: I just had never felt his hands before and it took getting used to. Be that as it may, it never happened again.

Apropos Cheng's ability in sensing hands, Lowenthal makes clear that his mastery didn't come from super-fast re-flexes: a seventy-year-old simply can't compete with young-sters on this—but from something else. Cheng often said that when he touched someone he immediately "knew" that person. It became obvious to me that he in some way was "hearing" his opponent's intent to move early enough to neutralize and counter it. The mechanism appeared to be super-sensing rather than super defensive reflexes. Recently, I read how scientist Benjamin Libet has found that when a person decides to make a small movement of his finger at an arbitrary time of his choice, a characteristic electrically-detectable change in his brain—called a readiness potential—occurs slightly less than half a second before he becomes aware of his intention to move (and of course still longer before he actually moves the finger.) The brain appears to have made the choice before the person is aware of it. This scientific evidence suggests that Cheng may have been able to hear the readiness potential sig-nal (his *Thirteen Treatises* go into some detail on this phe-nomenon).

This book is charming in its artlessness. In the welter of words and seemingly unstructured paragraphs and chapters there are large insights and little epiphanies put perfectly (for instance, noting Cheng's gentleness: "His delicacy resonated in that gentle place in me that I had blocked off for my adult life because I feared it wasn't manly. One of the many gifts he gave me was the way he led me back to the best part of myself.").

Throughout the text there is much talk of "it" in the sense of acquiring the essence of Taichi. I have often been asked by senior colleagues if I believed I had gotten "it." Unhesitatingly, I've said no. My answer may be skewed by the yardstick I used—Cheng himself. But though I may not have gained the skill, I understand now after thirty years what the essence—the British call it "quiddity"—involves. However that may be, this volume is full if "it."

So much so that I believe that if he read this spirited little volume, at the end Professor Cheng would smile his irrepressible smile and nod in affirmation.

Robert W. Smith
Flat Rock, N.C.
1991

Introduction

My teacher, Cheng Man-ch'ing, died in 1975. Even today I shy away from confronting memories of his death, but his teaching seems more alive than ever.

However, I think that there are aspects of his life and teaching which may be lost if they are not recorded. That is why I wrote this book.

Professor Cheng was called "Master of the Five Excellences": Tai Chi Chuan, painting, calligraphy, poetry and medicine. His favorite of the "five" was Tai Chi Chuan.

Professor Cheng was a true master of Tai Chi Chuan, and the fountainhead for the development of the art in the U.S. His influence grew from both the validity of his teaching and the awesome skill he demonstrated. Even well into his 70s, when Cheng Man-ch'ing talked about the "miraculous" qualities of Tai Chi Chuan, it was not "do as I say," it was "do as I do."

For a brief time Professor Cheng took up bowling. I never watched him, but it was fun imagining him in his robes flinging the ball down the alley. Then one day he announced that he had given up the sport.

"Why, Lao Shr?"

"I'm an old man, past 70. The ball was just too heavy for me."

The wonder of Tai Chi Chuan is that, theoretically, it should not involve any use of strength. Here was a man who could not roll a 12-lb. bowling ball but could send a 250-lb. man flying across the room with a touch.

He said, "You can lead a thousand-pound ox with four ounces, if you know the method."

I hope to share some insights into his "method" from my 22 years of study.

Professor Cheng was once asked, "What is the most important reason to study Tai Chi Chuan?"

"The most important reason is that when you finally reach the place where you understand what life is about, you'll have some health to enjoy it," was his answer.

More than self-defense, more even than its health benefit, he taught Tai Chi Chuan as a *Tao,* a "way of life."

Professor Cheng will be referred to in these pages as "Lao Shr," "Professor" and "the old man." I mean no disrespect, but I want to reflect the way we used to relate to him.

It is one thing to say of Cheng Man-ch'ing: "He is my teacher." It is my hope that were Professor Cheng to read this book he would say of me: "Yes, he is my student."

1

After two decades of study, I have begun to understand that Tai Chi Chuan is a spiritual discipline. For many years I had paid lip service to the concept, but the spiritual aspect of the discipline had no meaning for me.

Mark Twain wrote to the effect: "When I was 16 I was shocked by how ignorant my father was, how little he knew. By the time I reached 21, I was amazed at how much he had learned in five years."

I have a similar feeling about Professor Cheng and his teachings about Tai Chi Chuan – the old man has started to get pretty smart.

Many of us who studied with the Professor consulted with him about personal matters, as well as about matters of health and Tai Chi.

Once, early in my study, I suffered an emotional blow. After 10 years of slaving away at a typing job and writing unproduced plays, I co-authored a screenplay which began filming in Rome. The company that hired me had produced a dozen successful, low-grade action films and this was their attempt to break out with a "quality" film. Not only did I have one film in production, but I'd already signed to write a second. I was on top of the world.

Suddenly a combination of misadventures occurred: the Arab-Israeli war of '73, the subsequent oil embargo and stock market convulsion. The film's financing disintegrated; the company went bankrupt. My film stopped shooting barely three weeks into production.

I crawled back from Rome and collapsed into a chair next to Professor and told him the terribly depressing story. My dreams had died.

"Relax," he said. "Just relax."

He said more but it's lost to memory. I was dumbfounded by his basic advice.

"Relax?" I thought as I walked away. "What garbage. My life's in shambles and he's telling me to relax."

Years have passed. Emotional blows have come and gone, and I have begun to understand a key to living in balance: *we* are responsible for our lives. Not that there's anything we can do about a stock market collapse. We are "responsible" for our response to the flow of events.

Professor used to say, "As you grow more relaxed, you become less afraid. As you become less afraid you grow more relaxed." This is the nature of progress.

Any event in the world will produce suffering if one reacts to it fearfully, but if one relaxes and dissolves the fear reactions, one can meet even great catastrophes with equanimity.

I recently expressed this idea to a friend suffering through a horrendous series of family tragedies: "I can't accept that," she said.

2

There is a story of a samurai captain who after years of battles was assigned to the palace guard. There he looked up the Emperor's great sword master.

"Master," the captain said, "though I have been fighting for a long time, I've never had the chance to formally study the art of the sword. Would you accept me as a student?"

"Certainly," the sword master replied, "but first you must tell me what art it is that you are a master of."

"None," he answered, "I am just a soldier."

"Then study with someone else," said the sword master. "If you will not be truthful with me, I will not take you on as a student. I perceive that you are a master of some discipline, and I am never wrong about these things."

"Sir, I can assure you I am not lying," the samurai said, puzzled. "But perhaps I should tell you that after many battles I began to understand that the major problem was the fear of death. So I have meditated long on the matter, until finally I have reached the place where I no longer fear death. . . . Could that be what you meant?"

"Exactly," said the sword master. "Furthermore, there is no reason for you to study the art of the sword with me. There is nothing more I can teach you."

As a young boy Professor Cheng had an accident in which he suffered a near-fatal head injury. He was brought out of a coma by a wandering Taoist. For a number of years afterward, he was completely unable to concentrate and was feared to be permanently brain-damaged. Finally he was apprenticed to a master painter where, doing mundane tasks like grinding ink, he recovered his mental faculties. Still, he remained physically weak and sickly. While in his 20s, and already a renowned artist, he contracted tuberculosis.

His doctors predicted that he had six months to live; Professor Cheng took up the art of Tai Chi Chuan in a last-ditch effort to save his life. Soon he stopped coughing blood, his fever left and the tuberculosis was cured. He was still prone to ill health but would later consider that a blessing, because whenever he was tempted to give up the arduous study of Tai Chi Chuan, he would get sick and only the resumption of his Tai Chi would cure him. So he persevered.

He studied with the great Tai Chi master, Yang Cheng-fu, for seven years, practicing from morning to evening seven days a week. He often came home from the study hall so exhausted he collapsed, without the strength to lift his legs onto the bed.

He left Yang Cheng-fu after seven years. As a master of Tai Chi, Professor Cheng always gave credit to his teacher and to the illness which caused him to study and persevere.

There was another benefit of his near-fatal illness: "Since I thought that I would die, all my life since then I have considered to be a gift." The delight he felt and communicated to those around him was a result of the way he approached life: as one who has been reborn. Not with a sense of each day's weight, but with the knowledge of its wonder, that it is a gift to be alive.

Professor Cheng told us about his illness and "the gift of his life" many times, as if it contained a special lesson.

One difficulty in studying with a spiritual master is one's tendency to focus on the result rather than the process. In Lao Shr's case the "result" was his power, and the way he emanated the joy of a sage and a child.

We misunderstand the process. "Relax," he said, but there was something else, something not directly teachable. An idea that comes not to the mind, but to the "heart-mind," or the soul.

For a brief period I taught Tai Chi at Rikers Island prison. The class did not go well. Just prior to the class, "medication," primarily tranquilizers, was dispensed to the prisoners. One of them finally said to me, "Man, the last thing in the world we need is to be taught to relax."

People desperately pursue relaxation and the release from stress: illicit drugs, alcohol, caffeine, sex, television. There are a vast number of escapes, all predicated on the belief that life is too hard and that it demands relief. We think of relaxation as a way out, a retreat from the pain and pressure of our lives.

True relaxation embraces life, does not declare "time out" from it. We must accept that life is a difficult proposition, but like the soldier who "mastered" death, or Professor who saw each day as a gift, we can relax and find joy in life's challenges.

3

The first principle of Tai Chi Chuan is relaxation, without which there is no Tai Chi. The initial lecture Professor gave to each beginning class was on the importance of "relax."

"The whole body must be relaxed, loose and open, so that the *ch'i*, the vital energy, can pass through without blockage. This is the principle of Tai Chi as a health exercise, as well as a system of self-defense."

Later in the study, as we began to relax, he expanded the concept: Relaxation, he told us, is not simply becoming limp. There should be a quality of vitality about it. The beginner must focus entirely on letting go of tension and hard force, but, building on that foundation, the practitioner must contemplate the difference between going limp, which is lifeless, and the relaxation of a cat, which is completely vital and alert.

Once past the initial stage of just letting go, one encounters the substantiality of "relaxation." In push hands a beginner must concentrate on emptying out all resistance and hard force. Becoming "soft," alive to the *ch'i*, he will come to understand that relaxation is not becoming like jelly, but rather, as Professor described it, like becoming a bale of cotton: soft, but the more it is compressed, the firmer and more substantial it becomes. Even a bullet cannot go all the way through a bale of cotton. It will be absorbed by the substantiality of the softness. In addition, real relaxation is "heavy" while tension and hard force is the opposite.

The Chinese word *sung*, always translated as "relax," has the connotation of "looseness." When a shoulder joint is stiff like a hinge that needs oil, the arm and shoulder do not have freedom of motion; they are not *sung*. An arm that is loose, *sung*, cannot be put into a restraining lock; it will wriggle free like a piece of cooked spaghetti.

The same is true for the mind. When there is willfulness, a fixed preconception, the mind is not loose, not *sung*. Yang Cheng-fu said that the quality of the mind should be as spacious and all-encompassing as the expanse of the universe.

4

So important was the principle of relaxation to Yang Cheng-fu, he was supposed to have said "relax" a thousand times a day to his students. It was a word common to Professor Cheng as well, but there was one word he used even more often: "gradually."

Patience and Tai Chi. If you persevere in practicing the principles, achievement will come. You can't force it; you can't make it happen. "Gradually, gradually." You must be patient. On the other hand, mastery or progress doesn't rain down like manna on a lazy student. Arduous effort is required.

An apparent paradox: "Don't force" yet "Put in great effort."

In Tai Chi we learn Non-Action, the action that is not action. Non-Action is not really a great mystery. Everyone has experienced it to a greater or lesser degree: those times when we have struggled to create something, only to have it recede from us, until we give up. Then, if we are lucky, we tap some inner core of wisdom that allows us to take a deep breath and relax, and what we want seems to flow to us, or through us, like a gift from heaven, or more exactly, *as* a gift from heaven.

We must be patient, we must wait; but wait correctly, through the creative process of Non-Action. We make ourselves accessible—to the flow of *ch'i* in our bodies and the current of the *Tao* in our lives. The method is to eliminate blockages. There is nothing we have to *do;* that to which we aspire is already there. We must dissolve the blockages to let it emerge.

In the form and in doing push hands we must let go of tension and hard, stiff force to open up the myriad channels of the body to the flow of *ch'i*.

As for *Tao* in our lives, we have to learn to stop interfering with its flow. Take writing for example. Inspiration, the muse, is another way of describing the energy of Tao. You can't force it to come, but if a writer can let go of all the fears and fantasies that darken the creative present, learn how to get out of his own way, he finds that he is like a channel for that core of truth in the deepest part of his being.

Learning how to relax and let go is hard work, requiring perseverance and faith. "Gradually, gradually."

5

"The river of death has no lid on it. There are 10,000 ways to enter." – Professor Cheng

Tam Gibbs and Ed Young were Professor's two translators. They performed yeoman service at the *Shr Jung* school in New York, translating not just for the Tai Chi classes but for the 100 or so patients, most of them not Tai Chi students, who came to be treated medically every week.

Professor Cheng was a doctor of traditional Chinese medicine. Based on the flow of *ch'i* through the body and the balance of the internal organs, Chinese medicine was a complement to his Tai Chi. His primary method of diagnosis was "listening" to the pulses. Pulse diagnosis is described in the *Nei Ching,* the ancient classic of Chinese medicine. The practice is based on the concept that there is not a single pulse, but 12 subdivisions, each one informing the physician about the patient's internal condition.

At Tam's urging I had my first consultation – a general check-up. Professor Cheng's very soft fingers were on my wrist, and his eyes were closed. He told me that I had a cold around my heart.

I had given him no medical history but he was correct. A few years earlier I suffered an attack of viral pericarditis, an inflammation of the heart lining. I was bedridden for months, and when I finally recovered I was told the condition could recur. It hadn't, but whenever I was tired I felt something like an icy hand around my heart.

So he won me over with his diagnosis. I drank the vile-tasting herbal teas he prescribed for close to a year until "the icy hand" departed, never to return.

Professor's original school on Canal Street in Chinatown was divided into two rooms. Classes were held in the larger room. The smaller room, with his desk, some chairs and a table, served as a combination waiting room, doctor's office and general hang-out area. I spent much time in that room, listening for pearls of wisdom and, more important at the time, being an available partner for the "old man" should he feel like "pushing hands."

One day Professor walked away from his desk and, passing me en route to the larger room, pointed at a pimple on my forehead and shook his finger at me with an amused expression. I took it as a joke but Tam said, "He doesn't just do that for fun. If I were you, I'd consult him medically."

Professor checked my pulses and wrote out a prescription to be filled at a little apothecary in Chinatown. Those teas took quite a lot of getting used to, comprised of strange herbs, barks, dried insects and who knows what other unspeakable stuff. He rarely commented on his diagnosis unless the patient pursued it; I thought that was bad form and never did. On this occasion he told me, "This medicine will taste like the very soul of bitterness. After you drink it you will get a high fever. Get into bed, sweat the fever out and, after a few days, you will be all right."

It came to pass. The tea was the worst I'd ever tasted. I gagged it down and soon was flattened with a fever of close to 104°. It lasted a few days until I finally got up, weak as a kitten, but feeling fine.

Later that day I saw some friends and told them about

it. One was a medical student and she asked me if I had any other symptoms.

I had some unusual spots on the palms of my hands and the soles of my feet. They had emerged while I had the fever and though they were starting to fade, she could still see them.

She said, "It's all well and good to have faith in an old Chinese doctor and his herb tea, but these are classic symptoms of the early stage of syphilis, so if I were you I'd get down to the VD clinic and have it checked out."

This was in 1969. I'd only been studying with Professor Cheng for two years and I didn't have *that* much faith. Unfortunately, I was also leading the kind of lifestyle that made my friend's diagnosis possible.

I went without delay to the main VD clinic in lower Manhattan. After waiting with a vast crowd of the youth of America, I was directed into a doctor's office.

After a perfunctory examination, the doctor said, "The normal procedure is that we first give you a blood test. You come back in a week and if you've tested positive we start you on a series of three penicillin shots to cure the disease. However, with your symptoms, what I'm going to do is give you the blood test, but also start the penicillin treatment today instead of waiting until next week."

I got my blood test and penicillin shot, and a week later I was back at the clinic, holding my chart and waiting with the youth of America. My name was finally called and I went into the office. I handed my chart to the same doctor who'd seen me the week before. He didn't remember me from the hordes he saw every week. He glanced at my chart, then seemed taken aback. He studied it closely, looking up at me from time to time.

I was starting to get concerned when he said, "Well, I must tell you. I have never seen anyone with your symptoms test negative. But you turned out to be an exception; your test results are negative, so we don't have to continue the penicillin treatments."

I left the clinic and was sauntering down the street when it hit me. Syphilis! The scourge of western civilization! The cure found only after World War II with the discovery of penicillin! The old man, with his herbal remedies from a medical tradition perhaps thousands of years old, had cured me.

Five years later the school moved from Canal Street to a much larger loft on the Bowery. Professor's medical practice had grown; there were 50 people, or more, waiting to see him whenever he was at the school. He didn't get up to practice push hands beside his desk any more and I didn't hang out there very often, but one day I happened to be sitting next to Tam as he was translating.

Professor was listening to the pulses of a peaceful-looking, balding man of about 40. Professor turned to Tam and said, "This man really respects himself. He doesn't have venereal disease."

I left the desk and a few minutes later Tam came up to me. "Did you get what he was saying about that guy not having VD? It was like *everybody else he sees has it.*"

Professor was probably aware of variations of disease produced by an era of promiscuity, largely undetected by Western medicine. Disease is the culmination of internal imbalances that he could hear much earlier. The AIDS epidemic has caused me to remember that day many times.

Professor said, "The health of the nation depends on the seed. If the seed is unhealthy, what hope can there be for the race?"

His bias against sexual promiscuity wasn't just because of health. He would point out that ours is a society that believes in the quick fix: have a headache, take an aspirin;

emotional pain, have a drink; problems with a marriage, get a divorce.

Besides the unhealthy side effects of most quick fixes, what about the underlying causes of the headache, the emotional pain, the failed marriage? We have no sense of dealing with them. We've never had to, and we don't really know how.

Sexual promiscuity is no different than liquor, drugs or all the other addictions and compulsions we use to hide from ourselves.

6

"The philosopher Tsang said, 'I daily examine myself on three points: whether, in transacting business for others, I may have been not faithful; whether, in intercourse with friends, I may have not been sincere; whether I may have not mastered and practiced the instructions of my teacher.'"
— *Confucian Analects*, Chapter IV. James Legge translation.

Tam and I were alone at the school one afternoon, talking about his study of Chinese when Professor came in.

"Lao Shr," Tam said, "there's a word in this passage I'm studying that I don't understand. Here the translator has written 'friends,' but the Chinese word is not 'friends.' What is this word?"

Professor looked at the passage. "This passage is about what we are doing here, the study of *gung-fu*, the study of *Tao*.

"He asks himself whether each day he does three things:

"First, is he honest with people. He does not tell them lies.

"Second, is his heart open with—this is the word you want—'comrades in the same discipline.' This is the word you're asking about. You're right, it's not 'friends.' It's a different, special kind of relationship. It's what you two guys are, 'comrades in the same spiritual discipline.' It's a different relationship than friendship and in many ways higher.

"What he's saying here is that for you, it is not enough that you just be truthful, that you not lie, as if you were doing business with people. Here you have the obligation to go further. Your heart must be open. Tam, if you have thoughts about Wolfe, you must tell him, you can't hold them to yourself. It goes far beyond the obligation you have in normal relations with people.

"In the last part he asks, 'Daily, do I rekindle—like you would light a candle—do I daily rekindle the teaching that has been passed down to me?' Not just that you think about the teaching, but that it's alive. Even more, that it *burns*."

I have thought about that day and the Confucian text many times; thought about my inability to "open my heart." How many times, out of fear that I will be rejected, or that I will hurt someone I value, have I kept my thoughts secret?

In doing so, I deny my own truth. The resentment that builds inside me usually causes the relationship to deteriorate— the very thing I was trying to prevent.

Keeping my thoughts to myself also denies important, perhaps crucial, information for my "comrade's" growth. Even if someone would be hurt by my words, the fact that we are on the same spiritual path requires me to help him—and me— to become strong.

The obligation to help your comrade grow and become strong requires courage, but the "closed heart" denies itself the path.

7

"A person with an excellent sense of '*K'e Ch'i*' will be very good at Tai Chi Chuan." – Robert W. Smith (Bob Smith is one of Professor Cheng's most senior students)

K'e Ch'i means "manners," that characteristic of the Chinese that can be graceful when sincere and annoying when an empty formality. The etymology of the phrase is revealing. "*K'e*" means "guest." "*Ch'i*" is the same word – breath, air, spirit force – that is at the center of Tai Chi. So taken together, "*K'e Ch'i*" is "the air of a guest."

One could hardly have a better guiding principle. We are all guests. That we own and possess the world is the dominant, destructive illusion of "civilized" man.

Think of being a guest of the earth. Grateful, glad to be in this lovely house, respectful of everything which is, after all, not yours; but not subservient either, secure that your presence is welcome and provided for by a beneficent universe.

In doing push hands our attitude should also be *K'e Ch'i*. We should not try to dominate or overpower the opponent. Professor said that if your idea is to push or not be pushed, it is not Tai Chi.

The correct idea is to let the opponent have his way completely – we should not interfere with his energy. As a matter of fact, we empty out, allowing his force to proceed unobstructed; we even, ever polite, assist in the direction he so

17

eagerly wishes to go. Very self-effacing, very considerate. Like a guest.

If it happens that, as a result of our non-resistance and assistance, an aggressive person finds himself sailing through the air when his intention was to send *us* flying, we have not violated the principle of *K'e Ch'i*. Nature asks us only to stay balanced, and that is all we have done when the attacker sails away.

The Tai Chi form also expresses the attitude of *K'e Ch'i*. Think of our image of arrogance: chest puffed out, body rigid and hard, face frowning. Then think of the Tai Chi posture: body soft, energy dropping into the ground with the chest slightly hollowed, countenance gentle. The very attitude of humility.

Tai Chi proves correct the Biblical statement that "the meek shall inherit." That is an accurate evaluation of the outcome of a contest between arrogance and true humility. The uptight brittleness and floating quality of arrogance is no match for the person who has let go into the earth and can tap its power.

Although Professor Cheng rarely addressed the point, his teacher emphasized the idea of "floating" and its opposite, "heaviness." For Yang Cheng-fu, "heaviness" and "relaxation" were like two sides of the same coin. Relaxation allows one to sink into the earth, creating the root and substantiality of Tai Chi. Tension and hard, stiff force creates a lightness, a floating quality which is relatively weak.

On the psychological level, pride and arrogance are attempts to compensate for insecurity and feelings of inadequacy. A prideful person expends energy creating and maintaining psychological armor. It is a very brittle, weak condition. When a person lets go of the armor, learns to accept and operate his real self, energy is released and he grows stronger, and more creative and loving.

The "thank you" that we have been taught to exchange after a round of push hands often has the insincerity of *K'e Ch'i* gone wrong. We may try to emulate Professor's genuine graciousness but it's often a bad actor's imitation — a strained smile masking frustration and anger at an opponent who has been using strength to shove us around or willfully resisting when he's supposed to yield.

We miss the point of push hands and the "thank you." No matter how hard and unyielding our opponent, our inability to gently deal with him is indicative of our own stuckness. It is the exploration and eventual dissolving of the stuckness — not winning — that is the point of push hands. The "game" we really should be playing is with ourselves; we are coming face to face with the physical expression of the issues we hide from in our lives. In this confrontation with the self there lies the possibility of progress. We thank our opponent for providing us with this opportunity. If we really understood *K'e Ch'i* we would bow to anyone who "pushed our button" rather than become angry.

8

"Among the ancients, he who wished to have the shining virtue illuminated throughout the world, first governed his nation well. Wishing to govern his nation well, he first managed his family in good order. Wishing to manage his family in good order, he first cultivated his person. Wishing to cultivate his person, he first rectified his heart. Wishing to rectify his heart, he first rendered his thoughts sincere. Wishing to render his thoughts sincere, he first let his innate intellect reveal itself. The way to reveal innate intellect is to eradicate the desire for things." – Confucius' *The Great Learning*.

" . . . unable to eradicate the desire for things, one's person cannot be cultivated. This makes up the principle which goes through all things." – from Professor Cheng's commentary on the Confucian text

In Tai Chi we try to relax in order to open up to the flow of the *ch'i*.

Ch'i is transcendent energy, the life force. Professor said, "The *ch'i* that flows in our bodies is the same *ch'i* that moves the stars in the heavens." *Ch'i* relates to the circulation of the blood, but also to the energy of thought and spirit.

The reason so many people have the feeling deep down in their hearts that their lives are pallid imitations of their real potential is because it's true. Tension and hard, stiff force block the flow of *ch'i* in our bodies. We grasp after "things," creating tension and blockages in the spirit.

We stagger about in the arid desert of materialism, toward varied mirages. We desperately hope to get enough – money or status – to defend ourselves against terrors within, and the threat of our eventual dissolution. But it's to no avail. We have cast ourselves out, separated from the life force.

9

When I think of Lao Shr's teaching, it is often the little things that come to mind. Like his seemingly endless packages of Good Things Come in Three:

"What are the three most important things to a human being?

"In order of importance: Work, Relationship and Spiritual Discipline.

"Work is the most important because without food and shelter, a human being cannot survive.

"Relationship means man and woman. It is the second most important because without procreation, the race cannot survive.

"A spiritual discipline is important, but obviously less so than the first two."

His teaching, like *Tao* itself, came out of nature and the primordial wellspring of wisdom that is as old as humankind, an emanation of the understanding of what it means to be human on the most basic level, and to be part of the earth.

One time I was in his office while Lao Shr, Tam beside him, talked with an old Chinese friend. Suddenly, in an act so out of character it was shocking, Professor reached out and slapped Tam's hand away from where it rested over his

mouth. Tam blushed but Professor paid him no more attention and went on with his conversation.

The next day I was alone at the school when Tam came
in, without his moustache.

"What's going on, man?"

"Did you see him whop me yesterday? It was because of
my moustache. Won't let that happen again. You see, I had
this habit of playing with my moustache with my hand over
my mouth. To a traditional Chinese, when you cover your
mouth as you look at them, it's like you're judging them. Very
disrespectful. It's why he slapped my hand away."

Facial hair was something of an issue with Professor. He
laughed at how in China a person "earned" his beard while in
the U.S., surrounded by hippies as he was, men just grew them.
One of his own "earned" nicknames was "Whiskers Man."

He warned us against letting the facial hair extend over
the mouth, "bad for the *ch'i.*" When I cut off my beard and
shortened my hair out of an instinct to please him, he con-
gratulated me.

"You have taken off your mask," he said, "Very good."
He went on to tell me — only after I'd performed the deed —
that in China it was considered disrespectful to have facial
hair when your parents were still alive. "You don't want to
make them feel old."

This sense of consideration was as delicate as his touch
in push hands. Explaining how his favorite cat-whiskers writing brush had been made he said, "It's hard to make this brush
because you have to find many cats. You should only take
two whiskers from any single cat. A cat needs his whiskers
to feel his way in and out of tight spaces. Without his whiskers
the cat might get stuck."

In his book *Chinese Boxing, Masters and Methods,* Bob Smith
prefaces his chapter on Professor Cheng with a quote from

Bertrand Russell: "A civilized Chinese is the most civilized person in the world." The more I knew Lao Shr the more I appreciated how exquisite a description this was of him.

Once, early in my study, I was meandering through the maze of midtown subway tunnels when I ran into Professor with Tam Gibbs and Ed Young. Professor was standing a short distance away as I exchanged a brief hello with Tam and Ed. I glanced at him out of the corner of my eye. He stood in his traditional robe and skull cap, his eyes straight ahead. I felt something so forlorn about him in that moment; that graceful, powerful, wise old man stranded out of place and time on a grimy subway platform in New York City. Embarrassed, I turned and hurried on my way.

The next day Tam came up to me at the school. "Lao Shr wants to know if there was a reason, something the matter, why you didn't say hello to him yesterday."

It cut me to the core. I went to him and stammered out an inarticulate apology about how he seemed so self-contained I didn't want to bother him—but he never pushed me harder, and no single thing he ever did taught me more.

And for all the years he continued to teach me, I always greeted him when he entered and stood when he left, waiting for him to acknowledge the gesture of love and respect.

More than following the form of the idea, he pushed me to meditate on its substance.

In the 1960s rudeness was a political statement for many of the young. It was after all the establishment killing people in Vietnam who responded to the young protestors by calling them ill-mannered and disrespectful.

There is an insensitivity among many "well-bred" Americans, secure in their material advantages, toward the "ill-mannered" desperation and rage of those shut out from those advantages.

But taken as a whole, we are a society that is insular to a fault. We have erected barriers that on the surface seem like pride, but at the root are based on fear of our fellow human beings. We are developing a national style that treats manners and consideration as outdated virtues practiced by those too foolish to know better. We are losing the ability to be "civilized," gentle and sensitive to one another and to ourselves.

10

"The Three Fearlessnesses"—translation from Professor Cheng's *Thirteen Treatises*:

1. The fearlessness of taking pain: If a person is afraid to take pain, then there is no hope for progress. In the Tai Chi Chuan Classics it says, "The root is in the foot." If a person is afraid to take pain, it will mean that the foot cannot be dropped into the ground to grow root. There is also no doubt that such pain-taking is beneficial to one's heart organ and the development of the brain. The fundamental method for a person who has just begun to do Tai Chi is to take three to five minutes in the morning and the evening, alternating standing first on one leg then on the other. Gradually the time is lengthened, gradually the person sits lower. The mind should be put into the *tan tien*, and without forcing, even a little bit, the heart of the foot should adhere to the ground. When one is rooting, he should extend his middle and index fingers to hold onto the back of a chair or the edge of a table, in order to be stable. After a while, when that is familiar, he can take away the middle finger, using just the index finger for assistance. Eventually even this will become very stable and the person will not need to be assisted by his fingers anymore. Then one can utilize the "lifting hands"

26

and "playing guitar" as two positions for this standing (or rooting) discipline. The basic "preparation stance" is also the rooting exercise – the basic rooting exercise – for the complete *gung fu* of the person's "one unity with the ground." The "single whip" is the extending and opening discipline, with all the joints open. All of these positions greatly benefit one's health and one's self-defense ability. One cannot afford to overlook them.

2. The fearlessness to suffer loss: One of the basic principles of Tai Chi Chuan is to give oneself up in order to follow others. Commonly understood, to give in and follow others means that one will suffer loss. Therefore in the first chapter of my *Thirteen Treatises* I said that one must learn to suffer loss.

How does one go about learning? By listening to other people's attacks – not only without resistance, but without attempting to counter. One may pay special attention to four ideas: "sticking," "connecting," "adhering," and "following." Then one will be able to easily neutralize.

This is not anything that a beginner, or a careless person, can do. It is not easy for a beginner to suffer loss, but if a person is afraid to suffer loss, then it is best that he not take up the study. If a person desires to learn Tai Chi, he must begin with suffering loss.

To learn how to suffer loss one must understand that it is the same as not being greedy for gain. When a person is greedy for small gain, in the end he will suffer small loss. When he is greedy for large gain, in the end he will suffer great loss. Conversely, if a person is able to suffer small loss, in the end he will acquire small gain, but it's only when a person is able to suffer great loss that in the end he will have great gain.

When a person is wise, he must want to attain health and functional self-defense. In order to do so he must grasp Lao Tze's principle of "concentrating one's *ch'i* to become resilient." Can a person be like an infant? This is the principle of Tai Chi Chuan. This is the place from which the student must start to learn.

Let me repeat: "When one is wise, in order to attain the body of the discipline (health) and the function (self-defense) one must concentrate one's *ch'i* to become resilient like an infant." Achieving that, he has learned the wonder and the method of suffering loss. The essence is contained in the song: "Let great strength be used to attack me; that strength will be diverted as if a thousand pounds by four ounces." Then a person's resiliency has reaped its effect.

3. The fearlessness towards ferocity: Lao Tze said of a child lying alone in the wild, "A rhinocerous' horn will not harm it. A tiger's claw will not tear it. A soldier's sharp weapons will have no place to land. It is because the baby has no concept of death." Lao Tze also said, "There's nothing under heaven that's more yielding and more resilient than water, yet when it attacks stronger things, it always overcomes them." Elsewhere he said, "The most resilient under heaven overcomes the strongest under heaven." He is not talking about ferocious things like the rhinocerous, the tiger and the armed soldier. He stresses the quality of water, saying that nothing can overcome the most resilient. This is what is meant by, "If I have no body, how can any harm befall me? No matter how ferocious the weapons are that oppose me, they are no threat."

When there is fear, one's psyche, one's spirit and one's body—the atoms in the body—must also be tense. When there is tension, one cannot be loose or relaxed. If a person cannot be relaxed, how can he be resilient? When he is not resilient, he must be hard, he must be rigid. Therefore for one to really understand the principle of Tai Chi thoroughly, one must have the spirit of great fearlessness. Then it would be like Mencius' saying: "If the mountain of Tai should collapse right in front of me, my face would undergo no change of countenance." It is because I have cultivated the greatness of *ch'i*. This is also what Lao Tze meant when he spoke of concentrating one's *ch'i* in order to become resilient. When that is so, one will be fearless in the face of ferocity.

I have spent many hours mining the rich vein of wisdom in "The Three Fearlessnesses," and it seems like there is always more to learn from it.

1. Taking pain: Recently I've come across an interesting translation of this phrase: "tasting bitter." It reminds me of the medicine Lao Shr used to prescribe, "the very soul of bitterness." To heal and grow, we often need to suffer pain, to taste bitterness.

Ben Lo, who has probably gone deeper into "the fearlessness of taking pain" than any of Professor's students in this country, exchanged "no pain, no gain" for the more precise "no burn, no earn."

"How very puritanical," said a fellow student.

Not really. Paradoxically, the "taking of pain" is not self-denial. The "taking of pain" is an expression of *Tao* and is essentially about feeling good.

Increasingly, I am aware of how on the psychological level I am afraid to "take pain." As a result I have not confronted my root fears, the conditioning that has controlled my life and blocked me from my most joyful, powerful destiny. Instead of fully confronting those fears, I have shielded myself from them by acting out with drugs, drink, food and sex. I used such stimuli to try to mask my unhappiness.

As I have begun following the *gung fu* of "taking pain," I have come to realize that true happiness, strength and peace come from the pain of honest, courageous confrontation with the self.

2. Taking loss: this much can be said about life—it is like push hands. The more you try to resist a lesson, defending

yourself against your stuck point, the more you will be driven into the corner you're so desperately trying to avoid. Until it breaks you, or brings you to your knees. Until you start to get it.

There's no idea in Professor's teaching more profound than "investing in loss"; none more difficult to practice.

We are asked to let down not only our physical defenses, but the psychological ones as well: the rigid self-images and shields we've erected.

No matter how determined we are to let go, the mind rebels. We believe we need those defenses; without them we will be destroyed.

The causes lie in our subconscious sense of unworthiness. We believe that if we allow ourselves to be vulnerable and let another in, he will recoil in horror. Rather than flow from our truth and creative power, we hide, defend and manipulate.

We are asked to have faith and to dare. If we can't let go we will lose, and if we can only do it a little bit, we won't win very much. We are like the tourist who goes into the gambling casino secure that he will only play with a little spending money – then he is told he must mortgage the house, cash in the I.R.A., sell his possessions and put all the money on the table.

3. Fearlessness of ferocity: I used to believe that my bottom-line fear was death, extinction, the dark figure at the end of the hall, but I've come to believe that is all metaphor.

The bottom-line fear is of separation. We forget that we are a part of the *Tao* (God, Universal Love, or whatever term resonates for you). In that failure of memory resides all our fear, because if we are one with "the Great Mother" (to use Lao Tzu's term) there's no harm that can befall us. Even death

30

is a part of her embrace. The Great Mother is eternal, perfect and — beneath our amnesia — so are we.

Many students resist the notion that it is possible to be soft in the face of a violent attack. Perhaps it is that most of us feel so powerless in society; we carry such residue of frustration and anger. Whatever the cause, a prevalent image is that of the violent attacker who deserves death or worse at our hands, whether or not we're capable of delivering it.

"Fearlessness in the face of ferocity" also requires the old Confucian virtue: "Do not do to another what you would not have him do to you." Confronted by an attacker, or more commonly, by the image of an attacker, our tendency is to depersonalize and objectify. The attacker as monster. Not a fellow human being, full of fear and pain. We cannot see the small, hurt child beneath the raging image of the mugger — and who knows what subconscious parental images are being triggered at the same moment? These images produce tension, anger and fear, none of which are of any value in an appropriate martial response.

One of the principles of *Tao* is that the world reflects what we hold in our hearts. An angry person will live in a hostile, anger-provoking world, while a loving person will have a much different experience of the very same environment.

It is true that there are few capable of mastering their fear to the extent that they can respond softly to a violent attack. But it is both the paradox and glory of Tai Chi Chuan that the very virtues which many understand to be the secret of living — gentleness, sensitivity, compassion — are as well the secret of mastery of the martial art.

"So far to go," sighs the student.

Yet the goal is not in some far-off, inaccessible place. It's right under our nose, already present within us. We simply put our *ch'i* in our *tan tien,* let go of the physical and psycho-logical armor, and become "resilient as a child."

Professor told us that he once had a student who "got it" in less than a year. What was the secret of this special person who attained mastery in a fraction of the time it takes the rest of us?

"It was because he had faith," said Professor.

11

A good standard for a Tai Chi school is how involved women students are with push hands. Push hands is about using softness rather than strength; it is ideally suited to women. But in many schools, push hands classes consist of a gang of strong men blocking and shoving each other around while most of the women sit on the sidelines.

To be able to win with Tai Chi principles requires a great deal of time and effort. In the meantime, without proper guidance, a class commonly descends to its lowest common denominator, the domination of strength and aggression over softness and sensitivity.

Here is where many women find difficulty. Professor Cheng said that women are naturally much more gifted in Tai Chi. Their understanding of sensitivity and softness usually takes men years to achieve. However, it can take a decade for their talent to "pay off." In the meantime, in an insensitive push hands environment, they will be shoved around and, probably most frustrating of all, be "taught" by stronger men who assume that because they are winning, they must know more.

Applying the virtues of softness is frustrating and difficult. All sincere push hands students—men and women—must confront this problem.

At the end of my second year of Tai Chi study, I had an insight into what could be achieved through the art and what I would have to do to get there. I got a part-time job and became a Tai Chi "bum." For the next five years, in the company of two other "bums," I practiced push hands six hours a day, seven days a week. Avoiding the crude blocking and shoving most beginners indulge in, we were soft—if not in our bodies and psyches, at least in our practice.

During those five years we were constantly pushed by other students—even beginners. We swallowed our pride—not without considerable choking—persevered and found a gate at the end of that bitter path that opened into a courtyard no less difficult but somewhat less frustrating: we had become Tai Chi players.

Now I hear fellow students on the path, sensitive men and women, frustrated by playing with those obviously less sensitive and understanding who nonetheless push them around at will and against whom they are powerless. Most cannot take this ego-battering. Women complain: "I've spent all my life getting pushed around by insensitive men, and now you expect me to make a virtue of it?" Others lose faith in Tai Chi itself, since it seems that no matter how hard they apply the principles, it doesn't work.

Professor once addressed push hands students, "Getting all the strong people, and they push . . . and it keeps going on like that, and it becomes 'play, play, play' just a big game. But strength is not far off. It's not to be spoken of in the same breath as Tai Chi Chuan.

"What we're really about here is not a game at all but following Tao, studying the Tao. This is not a game, this is not 'play.'

"If you really want to study, the way to do it is by putting a strong one with a weak one, or a strong one with a woman. First one pushes and then turns about after a few tries and lets the other push. It's not a matter of a contest, which is what it gets to be with two stronger people. This way you can learn."

He described this idea many times. "Weaker with stronger" tends to take the strength out of practice; the stronger doesn't need it, and the weaker knows it will do no good. It doesn't remove the "bitterness" from practice—only subduing ego and will can do that—but it does put the study on a plane that focuses attention on the real work.

It's not two strong people shoving each other around, "play, play, play." It's two people unwilling to use strength or resistance; two people trying to be soft.

The method Professor recommended starts with the use of a wall. One person puts his back to the wall—his job is to practice neutralizing. The other faces the wall—her job is to push. The person doing the "pushing" tries to find her opponent's stuckness and unbalance him with a minimum of energy. She should not shove, because she is trying to awaken the internal energy, which she will only discover after she has exorcised hard, stiff force.

The person with his back to the wall does not push. He is practicing neutralizing, and he should not resist at all. He should completely neutralize all the incoming force *before he attempts to return;* he must not use his strength to block her energy and then shove her aside. After three pushes, positions are reversed, and he will practice pushing and she neutralizing.

If both players are sincere, the neutralizer will have to invest in loss. "Investing in loss" was one of the greatest lessons Professor had to teach. Since neutralizing is a great deal more difficult than pushing, the one practicing it is sure to "lose." However, understanding that you are practicing Tao—

and sharing that practice with someone who, when you reverse roles, will go through the same difficulty—softens the sting.

"For instance," Professor said, "take two people, and one person's *gung fu* [ability, level of attainment] is better than the other's. We're also good friends, and I push hands with you every day, and I let you push me every day. Say you push me a hundred times, but I'll have studied how you did it. That's the idea. I ask you, who do you think the advantage lies with at the end of this? In that case, do you have the advantage or do I? Think it over. Now, that hundred times that you have pushed me, although I've lost a hundred times, it ends up that I've gained. I've stolen your movement, and understand how to do it, and how to get away from it. So it's like you're teaching me. You've taught me 99 times for that one time I get away. Which one has the advantage then, you or I?

"That's how by undergoing a great disadvantage, you become advantaged. You have to understand this. It's more important than pushing for a thousand days."

12

A student was confused and wanted Professor's help. He had studied Karate prior to Tai Chi and wanted to know which of the form's postures would be best to assume in a fight. "Ward off?" he asked. "Play guitar?" What fighting stance would Professor recommend?

"Just like this," Professor smiled. He was in the posture already; it was the way he always seemed to stand. Relaxed, weight mainly on one leg, hands gently clasped in front of the lower abdomen. "Just like this."

"A fight," he said, "is a contract that takes two people to honor. A combative stance means that you've accepted the contract. In which case, you deserve what you get.

"In a fight only two things can happen. Both of them are terrible. One is that you will lose and suffer the unspeakable: serious injury or even death. The second alternative is even worse; you will injure or kill the other person. In which case you will have the law to contend with."

Occasionally Professor would amplify his thoughts about fighting.

In dealing with an attacker wielding a knife: "Think of it as a feather duster. If you have that idea, you will not be afraid, and you'll be able to deal with it as if you were doing push hands."

Every so often as I'm indulging my ego by resisting my partner's force in push hands I remember this business about the knife. "What would this moment mean if instead of his hands pressing on my chest, it was a knife?" It is an instructive thought.

In dealing with an attacker who has a gun:

"Here is the defense," he laughed, raising his hands in the position of surrender. Then, more serious, "That is, if the person with the gun is further away than eight feet. If he is closer he is lost because you can move faster than his mind can pull the trigger." Professor was speaking from the perspective of principle and the development of his own art, rather than from our level of achievement.

And what, he was asked, if a fight were inevitable?

"If a fight were unavoidable, using the techniques of push hands should be sufficient. Yield with an attacker's blow and then send him flying. After one or two times, any attacker will probably be discouraged from continuing the fight.

"However, if you are attacked by a group of men, or men with weapons, and they are seeking your life, then you should get mean. That quality comes more from the form than from push hands."

Senior student Lou Kleinsmith explained to me afterward: "If someone takes a swing at you, you ought to be able to push him away if your push hands is any good, and that should take the fight out of the attacker. But if he is trying to kill you it's going to take more significant discouragement. For instance, breaking an arm or rupturing an internal organ, and that kind of stuff is contained in the form. So, you see, it's a mistake to think of the form as exercise and push hands as fighting. In a certain sense it's the form that has to do with fighting, not push hands."

Generally, the Tai Chi practitioner never initiates combat, so he is in a countering position. But when a group of armed men is going to attack—or as Professor said, "they are going to attack someone weak and innocent whom you want to defend, in that case it would not be wise to await their attack. Your strategy should be to take the initiative, but utilize a feint to precede your attack, which will cause your opponent to tense up momentarily and give you the opportunity to attack successfully."

Professor Cheng came from a tradition that was much more fiercely martial than ours. In his early years as a teacher of great repute he was expected to take on many challengers whose "trying of conclusions" (as Bob Smith would say) was often extremely violent. Even as a student he only twice played with his teacher, Yang Cheng-fu. Each time he was left lying unconscious in the courtyard.

For all this, and possibly because of it, he was very gentle with us. With all his tremendous power and deadly ability, he never caused injury in the ten years he taught in New York.

13

Professor Cheng was called "The Master of the Five Excellences": medicine, painting, poetry, calligraphy and Tai Chi Chuan.

His interests and expertise extended even beyond these "excellences."

There was a group of students who would occasionally bring Professor flowers to see him practice his love of flower arranging. I have no sense of how good he was at it; his arrangements were beautiful, but the formal art of flower arranging is beyond my understanding. I was always awed, though, watching a man of his great power displaying utter delicacy as he trimmed and shaped his floral arrangements. His delicacy resonated in that gentle place in me that I had blocked off for my adult life because I feared it wasn't manly. One of the many gifts he gave me was the way he led me back to the best part of myself.

He also loved games. Gambling is a tradition on Chinese New Year, so one year some senior students joined him for some serious poker. At the end of the evening, when the winnings and losses were totalled up, Lao Shr was well in the red.

"It's very difficult," he explained, "playing with people who have no idea how to play poker. You can't figure them out."

When he played chess, he didn't have to make excuses. There was no one at the school with his experience in Oriental-style chess. He said that though he was a good player, his wife was better.

Once while he was playing chess in Taiwan, Professor's powerful student, Ben Lo, asked permission to test his internal energy. Still concentrating on his chess, Professor held out his arm. Ben struck it and nothing happened.

"Again," Professor said.

This time he looked up from his game and concentrated while Ben hit him again. Ben's arm went numb and it took a week before it returned to normal.

Feng Shui is the Chinese art of living in harmony with the earth. *Feng* (wind) and *Shui* (water) represent the flowing elements of nature; placing oneself in a favorable *feng shui* environment is thought to produce good fortune, peace and long life.

Considered by some to be mere superstition, the ancient art of *feng shui* is taken seriously by many Chinese. Professor was an expert, consulted by businessmen and home buyers anxious that their property harmonize with the flow of cosmic *ch'i*.

My initial contact with *feng shui* was the day Professor was walking with some students in Chinatown and passed a furniture store that had opened near a Chinese cinema he frequented.

"Do you think that store will be a success?" he asked.

"I don't think so, Lao Shr," said a student. He pointed out that the store was situated directly beneath the elevated subway tracks. The tracks were aesthetically displeasing, and the store had to bear up under the din and rattle of the subway every time it passed.

Professor disagreed. "That store has a dragon passing overhead. It's most favorable. The store will be a tremendous success."

The cardinal principle of *feng shui* is that *ch'i* flows through the earth in much the same way it flows through the meridians of the body. Expertise in the art means understanding how to harmonize and even manipulate the cosmic *ch'i*. If there was one thing the old man knew about, it was the *ch'i*.

"Knowing the *ch'i*" whether it be in *feng shui*, Tai Chi or Chinese medicine may or may not be science, but it is definitely art and is not easily attained. The fact that such expertise is hard to acquire caused Tam Gibbs, a man of great accomplishment and greater promise, to have his life cut off when he was in his early 40s.

Professor had died a few years earlier. Tam's dedication to his teacher led him to assimilate Professor's commitment to Chinese culture. When he came down with a sharp, persistent pain in his abdomen, Tam sought out a traditional Chinese herbalist rather than a Western doctor. It was a fatal mistake. Employing the traditional techniques that Professor used so well, the doctor misdiagnosed and mistreated Tam's appendicitis. The appendix burst, the pain temporarily subsided, and the poisons poured into his body while Tam thought he had been cured, as Professor had cured him so many times.

In the last years before his own death Professor shifted his attention increasingly to his beloved Classics, studying and writing treatises on Confucius and Lao Tzu. His commentaries on the *Tao Teh Ching*, titled *My Words are Very Easy to Understand* translated by Tam Gibbs, was published posthumously (after both their deaths) and is just one harvest of Professor's last years.

As for the "Five Excellences" themselves, he had been head of the College of Fine Arts in Shanghai, and his paintings and calligraphy were exhibited and sold in China, Europe and the United States.

Little of his poetry has been translated. Some poems Professor wrote in the U.S. which Tam translated were almost excruciating in their expressions of longing for the China he loved; they were completely without sentimentality or self-pity.

Of all the Five Excellences, Professor said that if he had to choose just one, it would be Tai Chi Chuan, "because of the way Tai Chi allows you to interact with people."

But his most outstanding art went without a title: it was what he gave to those who came in contact with him. He was an inspiration and a beacon; he displayed the potential of the human spirit, available to us all if we can release the blocks to our *ch'i*.

14

Professor Cheng first came to the United States when he was sponsored by a group of Chinese businessmen. They formed a Tai Chi association in New York's Chinatown and established Professor's school.

Professor said that the three ingredients for progress in the study of Tai Chi Chuan (another in those endless sets of three) are correct teaching, perserverence and natural talent.

Correct teaching is most important because without it no amount of effort will accomplish anything. Natural talent is by far the least important. A gifted student has certain obvious advantages, but the untalented need only work hard and it will come, as Professor said, "by a thousand efforts, rather than the talented student's single effort. But having gained it, it comes to the same thing." As a matter of fact, there is an advantage in lack of talent. The percentage of expert practitioners who started their study in dramatically weak, sickly condition is so high it cannot be accidental. Being weak, one has little strength to fall back on, so there is a greater tendency to open up to the *ch'i*. The weak peson is also like the turtoise in its race with the hare; without talent he must persevere.

Accepting that Professor's system gives us "correct teaching," and since natural talent is essentially irrelevant, the critical ingredient is perseverance. The initial Tai Chi Association failed because it undervalued that quality.

Professor's concept was to make Tai Chi Chuan, in his words, the "most precious jewel of Chinese culture," available to anyone who could grasp its principles and do the necessary hard work. If this meant Americans—the Chinese can be extremely chauvinistic—he would not turn them away.

Most of his original sponsors could not accept this position. They conceived of the school as a Chinese club where they would be endowed with Professor Cheng's great skill. Instead the school was soon overrun with eager, young, non-Chinese, most of whom were white. To the further distress of the Chinese businessmen, many of these white students were bearded, long-haired, scruffy hippies. They who had rented the loft, who had supported Professor's move, felt excluded from their own Association.

A few of the Chinese sponsors stuck by him and became some of his most dedicated and able students. Most of the rest dropped out. Their resentment festered until a time when Professor was away on one of his periodic trips to Taiwan, during which they locked the door and reclaimed the Association for themselves.

His loyal students trekked like orphans in and out of various sites until finally relocating at a new, much larger loft a few blocks from the original Association. Though the place was prepared beautifully for his return, and though the enrollment expanded considerably, something of the spirit of the school was irrevocably lost in the move.

It probably reflected something in Lao Shr's heart; still one more step in his seemingly perpetual series of exiles—

from China to Taiwan, Taiwan to the United States, and finally from his roots among the Chinese to the alien embrace of the white students.

Not that he complained. His dedication to Tai Chi left him no choice but to go where it would be full-heartedly accepted. He also believed that the very foreignness of his American students had its compensations; a fresh investigative spirit he thought would make the New York school his best.

He was not, however, naive about Americans. He said that we suffer from an attitude that makes it hard for us to understand *gung fu* — effort, discipline, dedication.

Americans, he said, think of a spiritual discipline like soda bought at a candy store. "I will take my 50¢, put it on the counter and buy a soda. And if I don't like that, I'll pay another 50¢ and buy another soda.

"What you don't understand is that learning a spiritual discipline is not like buying a soda. It is what you put into it that determines what you get out of it."

The intensity and quality of one's effort determines the value of one's Tai Chi.

Professor described the *gung fu* in Tai Chi as akin to building a stack of paper by laying down a single sheet each day. Each additional sheet seems negligible, but if you persevere over the years and decades a single sheet per day grows into an enormous stack.

Aware of our impatience, he shaped his teaching to make it more accessible to Americans. When he taught in China, Professor thought nothing of having a student work with a single posture at the beginning of the form for six months or more — "until he got it right." Even his first American students took almost two years to learn the form, but by the time he'd been here a few years, learning the form's basic choreography took approximately nine months.

46

There was an aspect of his teaching that would have been dispiriting were we aware of it. Professor did not believe in spoon-feeding. He would tell you something once, perhaps twice, but if you persisted in the error, for whatever reason, he gave up. Perhaps something might snap you out of it; there was always that possibility. But he was too busy to waste time with you.

It didn't mean he stopped liking you as a person — many continued to bask in the sunlight of his attention long after they'd been dismissed from that part of his concentration that had to do with transmitting the subtleties of the art.

Professor was a visionary and a creator. He saw himself coming to the United States to plant a seed, "the most precious jewel of Chinese culture." It would be up to his students, and his students' students, to develop the intellectual courage to grasp the idea, and the physical and emotional discipline to nurture it.

15

" . . . Let true affection and happy concourse abide in this hall. Let us here correct our past mistakes and lose preoccupation with self. With the constancy of the planets in their courses or of the dragon in his cloud-wrapped path, let us enter the land of health and ever after walk within its bounds. Let us fortify ourselves against weakness and learn to be self-reliant, without even a moment's lapse. Then our resolution will become the very air we breathe, the world we live in; then we will be as happy as a fish in crystal waters . . . " – Professor's dedication to the school at its new location, called the "Hall of Happiness"

Though the old man had his down moments (he never stopped missing his beloved China), "happy as a fish in crystal waters" describes the quality in him that drew us on through the frustration and difficulties of Tai Chi study.

Founded in 1965, his New York Tai Chi school had grown significantly in 10 years. By 1975 its enrollment was more than 200. In addition, countless thousands had studied for a short time and taken the brief experience into their lives.

It was not just Lao Shr's presence that made the school a unique place. From the beginning he was the lodestar for some of the most dedicated, able and intelligent martial artists in New York. Many of the students who started with Lao Shr in the 1960s were Judo, Karate and Aikido players with decades of experience, some of championship ability.

Unlike many other martial arts schools, where students study for a few years, acquire minimal skills and go out on their own, the serious students who came into contact with the old man remained with him. Where another school might have a teacher with 10 years' experience and his assistant with three, "The Hall of Happiness" had more than a score of advanced students each one of whom could (as many later did) head up fine schools of their own.

Prior to his last trip to Taiwan, Professor gathered his six most senior students. "You are my six pillars," he told them. "Together, the six of you equal me."

His tone before this last trip was disquieting. Though his personality still sparkled and his powers had not waned, at least in our eyes, a note of foreboding entered into his dialogue for the first time.

We were hearing statements like, "If you have any questions you had better ask them now. Because I'm not going to be around much longer." There was no indication that he was returning to Taiwan for good. He was just going for another visit, like the two he'd taken in the previous ten years. What was all this talk about "I'm not going to be around much longer?" He never said that before the other trips. With his power and vitality, he made us feel he'd be around forever.

It got so dramatic in the last weeks before his departure that people were glancing at each other apprehensively as the theme kept recurring in his talks.

"I'm going back to Taiwan because there are only a few of my old friends left. Most of them are dead now. I need to consult with these friends so I can finish my work on the Classics." It felt like the lights were dimming every time he talked.

Coupled with this was the sudden focus on organizational matters: structuring the school to run without him. Though it was prudent, since he planned to be gone for a year, he never did it before and he had been away as long.

He went back to Taiwan and we never saw him again. He suffered a cerebral hemorrhage, was in a coma for two days, and then he died.

After mourning him, the initial response to his death was a collective resolve to make him proud, an increased dedication to cultivating the art he taught us and building the school he established. Some of us even felt we were beginning to practice his ideas better after his death, waking up to the reality that it was in our hands, that he would not be there to do it for us.

For a brief time it seemed that his vision would be fulfilled, that the elder six would stand in his place and the school would become a great center for spreading "the most precious jewel of Chinese culture."

But it was not to be. There was a flare-up of ego and ill-feeling, and in a few years all that remained was the bare shell of the school while its substance had scattered to the winds.

Some students thought that the school's dissolution was inevitable. Without Professor's magnetism, the tendency for senior students to develop individual interpretations of the principles would have made cohesion impossible. This view saw the break-up giving senior students space to grow as individuals and, coupled with the unity they shared in spirit, would produce a much stronger "school," beyond the limitations of the physical space.

There is creation and destruction in the principle of the Tai Chi: life withers and dies, and from death's decay life springs forth anew.

There is also the injunction of the "Hall of Happiness," to "lose preoccupation with self." If the Tai Chi is unity, separation is its opposite. "Preoccupation with self" creates separation — the sense of the other as sinner or devil; even the sense that we are adrift, lost and alone in the dangerous ocean of the universe where we must always defend ourselves. Separation rather than unity — opposing the understanding that we are all one, a part of the life blood of all creation.

Separation has its companion emotions: loneliness, anger, guilt and fear. Unity brings with it feelings of peace, security, harmony and happiness.

In the absence of harmony, apply the principle of push hands; we don't look to blame the other, we look to ourselves. We also need to understand that separation and its attendant negative emotions are not to be indulged; that is a sign that we are out of balance and if not corrected will lead to even worse trouble. The organism, healthy and in balance, is meant to be "happy as a fish in crystal waters."

16

Tam once told me a story of riding with Professor on the subway, going to the school. An old Hassid got on the car and sat down a short distance from Lao Shr.

The two old-timers checked each other out. There they were in their archaic garb, living expressions of a tradition centuries old. After a few stops the Hassid left the car.

Professor turned to Tam, "What a strange-looking old guy."

One time a bunch of us were in his office watching one of the American moon shots on T.V. Professor was always prideful about Chinese culture and, spurred on by the T.V. commentator's chauvinistic exuberance, the conversation got around to America's huge lead over China in space technology.

"There's a practical reason why America got to the moon before China," Professor said. "I'll show you." He picked up a ball. "This is the globe. Here is the moon," he pointed to a spot above the globe. "Here is the United States right under it, and here, on the side below, is China . . ."

Lou Kleinsmith was standing next to me. "I can't believe he's going to say this," Lou said to me under his breath.

"Obviously," Professor concluded brightly, "since the United

States is closer to the moon than China, the Americans should get there first."

"He said it, he said it," Lou turned and ran out of the room, as if in panic.

Professor would often go to Low Library at Columbia University to study classical Chinese texts. He was sometimes accompanied by some of his senior students. One morning he posed a riddle to the group.

"In order to appreciate the good in a thing, it is necessary to understand the not-good. So, what is not good about Tai Chi Chuan?"

The students were all puzzled. Tai Chi is terrific. It's great for your health, it can cure diseases, produce longevity; it's great for self-defense, and it's relaxing to boot. No one could solve the riddle.

"What is not good about Tai Chi Chuan is that it is so very difficult to achieve," Professor said.

Recently, I've had cause to ask myself the same question about Lao Shr himself. I have been a participant in the dissolution of the great school he founded in New York—a result of petty politics. Now, as I look around at those of us who attempt to carry on his teaching, I am struck by how short of the mark we are—both in terms of our accomplishments in the art of Tai Chi Chuan, and more significantly, at the enormous gulf between his radiant spirit and our gloomy, fearful egotism.

What limitations in him as a teacher do these failures represent?

Or is he still teaching us, and beyond correct method, we must persevere, because "it is so very difficult to achieve."

17

Relaxation is the cardinal principle of Tai Chi Chuan. Next in importance are Professor Cheng's Three Treasures. "Follow the Three Treasures," he said, "and you don't have to worry about your practice being true."

First is the point on the top of the head, corresponding to the soft spot on a baby's skull. "You should imagine," Professor said, "that you are suspended from heaven by a string connected to the point in the center of the skull." Another image he used was to imagine "one's head pressing upward toward the ceiling."

He once said you could practice for 30 years but if you did not pay attention to the top of the head suspended from heaven, your practice would be wasted.

The importance of this first "treasure" has to do with the spine. If the head is completely upright, "suspended from heaven," the spine will be completely erect, with no jamming of the vertebrae. In Taoist physiology, the spine is "the Pillar of Heaven," with nerves and internal organs connected to it. Misalignment and compression of the spine are responsible for countless ills.

"If the pillar of heaven collapses," said Professor, "what hope can there be for a person's health?"

It is the spine's absolute straightness—a loose rather than rigid straightness—which allows the *ch'i* to flow up the spine to the top of the head. This movement of the *ch'i* is part of the final, transcendent stage of Tai Chi development, described as "enlightenment."

The Second Treasure is the "Bubbling Well" or "Rushing Spring," a point in the middle of the foot, slightly behind the ball. The Tai Chi practitioner should conceive of his weight dropping into the ground through the Bubbling Well, rather than any other point on the foot. It is called the Bubbling Well because after a period of diligent practice, a practitioner begins to experience the internal energy bubbling up from the ground through that point in the foot.

Understanding the Bubbling Well leads to what Professor called "one's unity with the ground." The power in Tai Chi is an expression of the body's entire energy unified with and flowing from the earth. Though the energy is soft—only softness can develop the unity—it has the power of mass integration, like the individual droplets of water in a tidal wave.

Occasionally a student complains about pain in the ankle or knee. If the weight does not fall into the ground through the center of the foot, it will lock in the ankle or knee joint which is forced to support the weight. Pain is the joint's protest. The problem can usually be solved by the student concentrating on the Bubbling Well, allowing the joints to serve their natural function of channeling the weight into the ground.

"Further, if the foot is not connected to the ground, it will not take root," as Professor said. The root is part of the functional aspect of Tai Chi, allowing the upper body to be insubstantial and pliable while the legs are rooted in the earth. Professor described the "foot taking root" as a literal rather than figurative idea: "After a time your root will come to extend an inch or two into the ground. When your *gung fu* deepens, your root will extend to a depth of several feet."

Root enables the Tai Chi practitioner to yield to an opponent's force, allowing it to pass through without being knocked over. It is like a palm tree in a hurricane: the trunk pliable and yielding while the roots are firmly connected, so that the tree is not swept away for the force of the wind.

The process of the foot taking root ensures the development of great strength in the legs. In Western medicine the legs are called "the second heart." The health and vitality of dedicated Tai Chi practitioners at an age when most others are infirm is a partial expression of the strength of the circulatory system, and the legs.

But it is more than simply the strength of the heart and legs that accounts for the vital condition of aged Tai Chi practitioners. According to Professor, it is the nurturing and development of the *ch'i* that produces the wonders of Tai Chi Chuan.

Third and most important of all of Professor's Three Treasures is that which directly bears on the development of the *ch'i*. Professor said that if one practiced the *gung fu* of this third treasure, one would not need to practice any of the rest of the discipline.

This most important point is the *tan tien*, "the field of the elixir." It is a point approximately an inch below the navel, 3/7 of the way from back to front. It is where the *ch'i* is gathered and nurtured, until it eventually overflows into body and bones: the body filling with "spirit" *ch'i*, becoming relatively impervious to blows and many illnesses, the bones becoming "hard as steel" rather than the brittleness that comes with aging. Finally, the *ch'i* travels up the spine to the brain, where it comes down as "the golden rain," enlightenment.

56

To nurture the third treasure one must, in Professor's phrase, "Keep the *ch'i* and the heart/mind mutually guarding one another in the *tan tien*."

Though literally translated as "breath," *ch'i* has a range of meanings to the Tai Chi student. According to Professor Cheng, there are three kinds of *ch'i* that gather in the *tan tien*.

First is the breath, air, the "*ch'i* of heaven." Second is the *ch'i* that comes from the blood, "the *ch'i* that we get from our parents." Third is the "*ch'i* of the internal organs."

The "heart/mind" which "guards the *ch'i* in the *tan tien*" is almost as foreign an idea as the *ch'i* itself. In traditional Chinese physiology there are two kinds of mind—the rational, problem-solving mind, and the heart/mind. The heart/mind is intuitive, relating to feelings, and is considered to be more reliable than the other.

These categories parallel the Western idea of the brain's division into left and right hemispheres, with the "left" brain performing the rational functions, the "right" brain the more intuitive. Even the "more reliable" quality of the heart/mind has a parallel in the Western theories of the "right" brain's connection to a "higher consciousness."

The *ch'i* of the air, the breath, is gathered with the heart/mind in the *tan tien*, where it is joined by the *ch'i* of the blood and internal organs. Then an alchemical process takes place. After a time of the *ch'i* being "cooked over the fire" of the heart/mind, it is transformed into a kind of steam which overflows the *tan tien*. This "steam" is the fourth kind of *ch'i*, the "spirit *ch'i*," which permeates the bones, fills the body and travels up the spine to the brain.

The benefit of the "*ch'i* and heart/mind mutually guarding one another in the *tan tien*" cannot be hurried or forced. Without relaxation it cannot take place.

"Relaxation" and the "Three Treasures of Cheng Man-Ch'ing" form the guideposts of Tai Chi Chuan. Following them, a student's practice will deepen. Any question about Tai Chi Chuan is best examined in terms of its relationship to Relaxation and the Three Treasures.

18

"In the application of Tai Chi Chuan, when it comes to the point of someone wanting to hit me, or to attack me, then the real usefulness of the art makes itself known. For instance, take a piece of cloth. You can beat it but you won't harm it. It doesn't resist you, it's not stiff. So if you're as soft as the cloth, then there's no problem. Moreover, one who is soft will not be afraid when people come to attack. Then you will be able to respond to an attacker's speed and strength in an effective manner.

"The first and most difficult point of all is: you have to believe in what I say. If you don't believe it, when the person comes to attack you, you will resist him and then it will already be too late." – Professor Cheng, translated by Tam Gibbs

Again: the crucial article of faith – the practicality of softness.

The "difficulty" is that softness is a quality of the true self, that which exists beneath our myriad defenses.

Resistance is rooted in our lack of faith in the self. We create armor to protect that self from the world: hard images of strength and brittle, false fronts. These images exact a huge toll of energy required for their maintenance.

Because of this psychic armor, we are blocked from creating or loving, and the awareness that we are living a lie compounds the fear and self-disgust.

The *gung fu* is to be soft, to let the armor drop, and relax down to the gentle, tender self that exists beneath it.

"The first and most difficult point" would probably be impossible were it not for the wisdom of the heart. The heart knows that the *gung fu* of softness is not only practical, it's the only path worth taking.

19

Mastery of the art of Tai Chi Chuan is difficult; one of the functions of push hands is to remind us how far we have to go. There are aspects of Tai Chi in which it is easy to deceive oneself in regard to attainment — not push hands.

A common misunderstanding is that push hands is the martial part of our *gung fu,* something like Tai Chi sparring. The three basic components of Professor's Tai Chi are the form, push hands and the sword. Each in its own way is about health and martial ability.

The growing number of push hands tournaments, and the attitude behind them, is a dreadful development. Push hands is not the strong dominating the weak, the fast gaining victory over the slow. It is the subduing of the will to achieve understanding of softness, so that a slight, 75-year-old man, completely relaxed, can with a touch send a 250-lb. Judo champion flying. Doing push hands competitively invariably debases the art. Tournaments engender bullish individuals straining and sweating as they try to shove each other out of the circle. Not only are the Tai Chi principles absent, but what is left is absurd. As Bob Smith said, a good Sumo player could go through one of these Tai Chi tournaments like wind through wheat.

Tai Chi done well is the best of the martial arts, and done badly it is the worst. Under the growing influence of the competitive attitude, the scale of Tai Chi is tipping in the wrong direction.

Another price a student pays for doing bad push hands is the lessening of martial ability. "Function" in Tai Chi comes via osmosis, from diligent practice of the principles. It is not so much the acquiring of techniques as it is the restructuring of body and psyche, "the very atoms of the body," in order to be "resilient as an infant." Doing push hands as a blocking and shoving match accomplishes none of the internal changes necessary.

20

It is easier to criticize bad push hands than to practice or even describe the good. The secret, simple but not easy, consists of four Chinese characters: "Don't Resist, Don't Insist," or the sentence, "Don't use more than four ounces nor let more than four ounces build up on you."

Professor's injunction was "Study the [push hands] form, it has meaning!" The epitome of impatience on this point was a system devised by a benighted fellow who taught Tai Chi on Long Island. He had two push hands classes. The first class held perfunctorily to the push hands form; then in the teacher's words, "we take off our shirts and get into some serious pushing," without the form's perceived limitation on good wholesome play.

"Study the form, it has meaning!" *Pung, Lu, Chi, Ahn;* Ward-off, Rollback, Press and Push; the postures of "Grasping the Sparrow's Tail." In push hands the postures should have exactly the same quality they have in the form: back straight, arms loose and relaxed, body completely devoid of tension and hard, stiff force.

Push hands develops understanding of energy and balance. The goal is to enable the practitioner to deal with any kind of attack or energy statement, not just someone playing the same game. But the method lies in mastering the push hands form.

Professor said, "Don't Ward-off into the opponent's realm, nor Rollback into your realm." If I Ward-off "into the opponent's realm," I have over-extended, and that vulnerbility will result in defeat by a skillful opponent. "Over-extension," in Professor's words, "is a position that is asking for a beating."

"Doing Rollback into my realm" means that I have allowed my form to collapse. Rather than turning aside, deflecting the opponent's energy, I have permitted it to strike home. Rollback is the quintessential Tai Chi posture, the essence of the functional principle. Professor describes Rollback as "setting a trap." Since a Tai Chi practitioner should normally never initiate combat, this puts us in a position of responding to an attack. That response is to Rollback, to deflect the opponent's energy, and having led him on, allow his greed to result in the over-extension that we use to send him flying. The push generally follows up the successful Rollback: the opponent's attack having failed, he retreats to gather himself for another attack; we follow, add energy to that retreat, and push.

"Listening" is the technique of the push hands practitioner. Here is another reason why blocking and shoving is counterproductive. To listen one must be soft and relaxed. Listening leads to skill in "Sticking," the key that opens the gate to push hands, as well as the wonder of Tai Chi Chuan as a martial art.

Professor's words on the fighting aspect of Tai Chi are disappointing to those searching for specific techniques. He focused almost entirely on the idea of Sticking. If you really understand Sticking, said Professor, you have achieved martial proficiency: If you are "soft as a piece of cloth" a blow will have no point upon which to exert force—it takes two hands to clap. You will also be able to "hear" the opponent's intention before even he is aware of it, thus putting him completely at your mercy.

The highest level of Listening and Sticking is what the old man called "Receiving Energy." This is where the practitioner transcends the basic techniques of push hands, the need to either neutralize or push. The opponent's energy is "received" and instantaneously returned, like a tennis ball bouncing off the resilient cords of the racket. At its highest level, Receiving Energy enters an ineffable realm, where as a result of what Professor calls the practitioner's spiritual enlightenment, he is able to repulse an attacker "with a look." The old man stressed that this level of attainment is not magic; it is real and something we can achieve.

Before we transcend we must apply our intelligence and discipline to mining the depths of the push hands exercise.

Professor's push hands classes usually began with a long row of students playing together. Professor would walk down the row and almost invariably make two corrections: he would place his hand on the base of a student's sacrum and thrust down and forward, persuading the sacrum to "drop." Then he would take the players' elbows and hold them together, elbow joint to elbow joint, looking you in the eye as if to say, "Dummy, now get this, this is important!" Then he would walk on to the next pair while like recalcitrant children behind the teacher's back, our sacrums would pop back and our elbows separate.

He emphasized the sacrum and elbow because they form the keystone of the exercise. There is a Confucian principle which Professor characterized as the straight line connecting heaven and earth. This line, which also represents humankind, is the principle of centeredness, balance and moderation. The "dropped sacrum" with its corresponding erect spinal column is the expression of this centeredness in push hands—without it the posture is "broken." The opponent's attack cannot be turned aside nor can the energy of the ground be tapped for the correct push.

The maintaining elbows in contact forms a leverage point that allows the pivot of the straight sacrum and spine to affect the opponent's energy. Otherwise, you might turn in response to an attack, but lacking the leverage point, the opponent would not be sent flying. You would understand what Joe Louis meant by, "He can run but he can't hide." It is the dropped sacrum and elbow in contact that make all the sensitivity and sticking function.

Of the two aspects of push hands, neutralizing and pushing, neutralizing is much more difficult. Neutralizing is not simply evading an attack but is a simultaneous emptying out and filling up, evading and returning the attacker's energy back onto himself.

Visualize a circle with you, the neutralizer, at the center. The opponent is on the periphery and his intention is to push through the center, thereby defeating you. Your job is to keep him on the periphery. Your method is to hear his energy, yield and turn. It is as if the opponent, trying to push you, enters a revolving door. Instead of going through the center, your pivot point, he spins on the outside, one door giving way before the push while the other simultaneously "fills up" behind him.

To push is somewhat easier but still hard to do well. Your goal is to go through the opponent's exact center. If you miss to the left or right, up or down, you will allow the opponent's axis to rotate and the effect of the push will be dissipated; if there is any excess energy, you will be pushed. If the direction of the push is correct and the internal energy is applied, the opponent will take off like an arrow shot from a bow. No one who has ever experienced a good "push" will ever think of Tai Chi as a strictly defensive art.

The Tai Chi Classics describe two kinds of energy: hard/external and soft/internal. Soft energy is immensely powerful. It is a paradox that small children and animals use soft energy, while adult humans normally use the less efficient, hard energy.

Hard energy blocks the flow of *ch'i*; it is a disjointed expression of a fraction of our potential strength. It is commonly the strength of the arm from the shoulder to the hand, and part of it always remains locked in the body of the one using hard energy.

The soft energy is consistent with and does not block the flow of the *ch'i*. Rather than being disjointed, it is connected. The energy flows from the ground through the whole body. It represents the power of the entire body; Professor characterized it as being like the massed effect of wind or water in a hurricane or tidal wave.

A good push is not just an expression of internal energy. As the practitioner becomes soft—developing his internal energy—he also grows sensitive. He learns to find the opponent's center. This is a very subtle process; it involves "hearing" the precise quality of the opponent's imbalance and the direction of the push, as well as, in Professor's words, "detecting the first wave of resistance." As the opponent retreats, you "hear" as he begins to get stuck before he himself realizes it; at the instant he begins to subconsciously resist retreating further, you withdraw and follow with the push itself—a short, unified expression of energy, the power coming out of the ground, sprouting in the legs, directed by the waist and emerging from the hands, which should move no more than an inch.

There are two methods of pushing an opponent: to push the "empty spot," or *ti fong* (the withdrawal-attack technique) the "hard spot."

One of the principles of *yin* and *yang*, hard and soft, is that when there is a stuckness in the body, a hard spot, there will also be an indefensible, counter line of energy—a soft spot. With two hands on the opponent, the attacker "hears" the resistance at the place the opponent is defending, the hard spot. At the same moment the attacker will also hear a counter line of energy that the opponent cannot defend—the soft spot. Both the hard and soft spot are vulnerable to the push. Which one is chosen depends on conditions of strength and the relationship of the opponent's stuckness to the attacker's energy.

In order to push it is necessary to understand a basic law of the internal energy. It is a simple but crucial point: the full or substantial hand is always opposite the leg bearing the majority of the weight. So if my weight is anywhere from 51% to 100% on my left leg, my right hand is full, and vice versa. It is the full hand that must be used to release the internal energy. Applying energy counter to this basic principle is called "double weighting" and is a fundamental error. A double-weighted attack is always imbalanced, disjointed and can never tap the energy from the ground.

When we attack with the internal energy, we are not attacking with the left or right hand, but with a line of energy that originates in the foot, is channelled through the legs, waist and back, and only emerges from the hand.

One additional problem: where the soft spot is vulnerable, the hard spot is not. My attack can always go right through the soft spot, but if I attempt to do the same thing to the hard spot, I will be blocked by the resistance. So

I must use the withdrawal-attack technique, the *ti fong*.

At the moment my opponent starts to resist—his first wave of resistance—he presses back against my hands. At that instant he begins depending on my energy for his balance. If I should withdraw, he totters forward. While he is tottering, his root and balance are broken. He cannot resist and is completely vulnerable. At that precise instant, after the ever-so-slight, delicate withdrawal, I attack, releasing the arrow of my energy. This entire process takes place in a fraction of a moment, in the smallest of spaces. It requires soft, rooted energy and great sensitivity. It is one of the wonders of Tai Chi—the epitome of Non-Action—a push with no willfulness or hard force but with lightning-like speed and power.

One of the reasons push hands is so difficult is that it is permeated with this principle of Non-Action. The push hands player does not try to push or defend. His attitude is that he follows. In no way should I interfere with my opponent's energy. I give him what he wants while creating the condition where what he gets is not what he expected.

To do it successfully, I must be balanced and alive. In the words of the Tai Chi Classics, I become like a balance wheel, so sensitive that should a fly alight on it, it would be set in motion.

My attitude is one of listening, without intention. If there is intention I lose my sensitivity. I cannot both "do" and "listen." "Listening" comes from Non-Action. It is just "being there," without will or predetermination.

In the push hands form, "giving the opponent whatever he wants" means that there is no moment that is automatically *yin* or *yang*. If I am doing the exercise correctly, the meaning of each moment is determined by my opponent's intention. It is a mistake to believe that individual postures in the push hands form have intrinsic attack or retreat qualities; for instance, that Ward-off recedes or that Push attacks. In fact, every posture has the implicit capacity to attack or neutralize; it depends on whether the opponent is heard to be attacking or retreating. "The choice is his, the power is mine." In principle, hearing the opponent's intention should result in his defeat: "The battle is over when the swords cross" is a saying in Chinese fencing.

"What do I do if my opponent doesn't move?" is a question beginners often ask. It is a statement of insensitivity. "Listening" means the ability to not only understand overt movement, but even the implicit energy in an apparently static position. The protest, "What do I do if he doesn't move?" is usually applied to a situation where a beginner is dealing with a stubborn, resistant opponent who refuses to budge. The beginner tries to "push" but the opponent, ox-like, is immobile.

But the beginner shouldn't be pushing, he should be listening. If he were, he would hear that his stubborn opponent is not really static at all. The nature of all resistance is that it *presses back* against a real or imagined force. Were our beginner to draw the stubborn opponent forward slightly—going with the resister's energy, and counter to his expectation— the beginner would have his opponent off-balance and at his mercy.

The objective in push hands is to grow more neutral, softer and sensitive, to hear my opponent's intention while he has no idea of mine. When in the position of Push, I should not exert force. That would be like sending him a telegram, giving him something to work with. I should be neutral and allow him to lead me to the place where he is stuck, which you can depend on him to do, if you are patient. Only when I hear his stuckness do I send forth my energy.

"Giving the opponent what he wants" will for a considerable time result in him getting exactly what he wanted – you will lose. Until you learn "the wonder of the method," you must be prepared for long and bitter defeat. It is the only path to progress. "If you are greedy for gain in the end you will suffer loss . . . Only if you are willing to suffer great loss will you have in the end great gain."

21

"This is not a game. What we're really about here is the study of *Tao*." — Professor Cheng

"Tai Chi" is commonly translated "Supreme Ultimate" (hence we get the prideful and totally non-Taoist "Supreme Ultimate Boxing"). A better translation is "Great Polarity," as in *yin-yang*, male-female, positive-negative, the abiding principle of the universe. "Chuan" is literally "fist," or "system of self-defense." So: Tai Chi Chuan is the system of self-defense based upon the principle of the great polarity.

Tao is indefinable. There is a passage in Lao Tzu's *Tao Teh Ching* that says, in effect, "the person who knows the *Tao* does not speak it." With that warning the reader can take the following words for what they're worth.

The literal, narrow meaning of "Tao" is "Way," as in "road" or "path." In literal terms *Tao* is the way to get from Pittsburgh to Cleveland, or from birth to death.

A more fundamental description, like *Tao* itself, has to be gained between the lines, a mystery partially revealed as we chip away what-it-is-not and discover its laws.

Is there anyone who hasn't had the experience of desperately wanting something—job, money, lover—and see it further recede the more we want it? But if we can somehow dissolve the desperation, the thing we thought we wanted flows to us like magic. As a fellow student put it, "Oh, one more case of my getting something after I no longer want it."

Tao does not seem to be something we need to acquire. We are already a part of it. We can, however, do a great job of blocking its manifestation within us. We primarily block the *Tao* through fear and tension.

To experience *Tao* we have to be open. In push hands if I am not completely receptive to my opponent's energy, if I have a preconception of what I want it to do, if I try to block or manipulate it, I am inaccessible to *Tao*.

If a lonely man walks down the street, longing for a lover to cure the pain in his heart, he will wear out three pairs of shoes without easing his troubled mind. If he can detach himself from the fear that exists beneath the longing, the fear that he is no good and incomplete, he can accept that he is OK right now and at one with all there is and ever will be. Then he will exude positive energy and his smile will be warmly returned up and down the block.

It is the law of *Tao* that what you put out is what you get back. If I am open, generous and loving, I will experience life as safe, abundant and full of love. If I am tense and fearful, and view life as dangerous and hostile, my life will reflect that fearful reality. How could it not? I have defined the terms and placed myself within the gestalt.

The *Tao* feels good. Are we having fun? Or do we feel angry, jealous, lonely and guilty? If we are in pain, we are not relaxed and we are resisting; we have blocked the flow.

Fear is the source of the blockage; it underlies our painful, negative emotions, even though its presence is usually hidden.

A friend resigned from her job. "I liked the job but there was too much pressure, I couldn't take it."

"What kind of pressure?"

"They always made me feel that if I didn't perform perfectly, I'd get fired."

She was afraid she would lose her job. In order to placate the fear, she quit her job. The kind of "perfectly rational" thing we do every day.

What else could she have done? She could have relaxed. Perhaps they *were* pressing her to do it perfectly; but perhaps, out of her own lack of self-esteem, the *fear* that she was not good enough, she created the pressure she couldn't handle.

She could have let go, saying to herself, "Since I like this job, why don't I just stop worrying about doing it 'perfectly' and just go with it, have fun. If they fire me, they fire me, but in the meantime I'll be doing a job I like, having fun with it, and who knows what tomorrow holds anyway?"

Fear blocks *Tao* by warping our perception. It sends us guiltily into the past or anxiously into the future, rather than letting us relax in the present.

Professor once said, "Do push hands as if you were standing on the edge of a cliff."

The students' immediate response was to stiffen up and resist. "Damn! I sure don't want to get pushed off a cliff."

That's not what he meant. There is a Zen story about a man chased by two tigers. Trapped at the edge of a cliff, he seizes a vine and lets himself over the side. As he hangs on the side of the cliff he sees a tiger above him at the top. Looking down he sees the other tiger waiting for him at the bottom. Then two mice begin chewing through the vine from which he hangs.

At that moment, with his life in the balance, he sees a wild strawberry growing out of the cliff wall beside him. He picks the strawberry and eats it, thinking how delicious it tastes.

Push hands is not a game, it is the study of *Tao*. Therefore it should be played like you're standing on the edge of a cliff, or suspended on a vine between two tigers, in a crystalline moment between life and death. We can waste our short time on the vine fretting away our life, or we can let go of our fear and enjoy the strawberry.

22

Professor taught that there is a vital connection between Tai Chi and the Classics that forms the foundation of Chinese culture. Tai Chi is generally thought of as a Taoist art. Its legendary originator, Chang San Feng, was a Taoist priest who lived in the 13th century.

Professor said that he was 30% Lao Tzu, the Taoist sage, and 70% Confucius.

Professor said that the third chapter of Lao Tzu's *Tao Teh Ching* is crucial for Tai Chi students. Here is Professor's version of the critical passage with excerpts from his commentary, translated by Tam Gibbs. It is different from most other translations, revealing the substance beneath what for other commentators is abstract principle.

> That is why the Sage governs himself
> by relaxing the mind,
> reinforcing the abdomen,
> gentling the will,
> strengthening the bones.

"'Relaxing the mind' is the doctrine of non-action. 'Reinforcing the abdomen' means, in the words of the Yellow Emperor, 'the Sage swallows the Breath (*ch'i*) of heaven to reach spiritual enlightenment.' In Chapter 20 it says, 'prize the food of the Mother.' 'Mother' is the mother of all living things, the life-giving 'Breath' (ch'i) of heaven-earth. This is the Tao of Lao Tzu . . . . If one were to say that the way the Sage governs himself were no more than to fill the belly with food, how could Lao Tzu's *Tao Teh Ching* be worthy of its title?"

For Professor the essence of Tai Chi Chuan is contained in the phrase, "Let the *ch'i* and heart/mind guard each other in the *tan tien*." Here is the profound benefit of Tai Chi: the process whereby the *ch'i* gradually gathers in the abdomen until it eventually overflows, filling the body and producing health, power, vitality, and even the "magical" reversal of the process of aging. As we get older the bones normally become weak and brittle; through nurturing *ch'i* in the *tan tien*, the *ch'i* eventually enters the bones which become, in Professor's words, "essentially hard, like steel."

The relationship of Confucius to Tai Chi is probably most present in the push hands exercise. "Lao Tzu," Professor said, "is for the sage, living alone on the mountaintop. My aspiration is only to become a human being, learning how to live in the world with my fellow humans, and this is the object of Confucius' teaching."

If the form parallels the lone Sage atop the mountain nurturing his *ch'i*, push hands mirrors the relationship between humans in the world. The dominant themes are Balance and Justice.

Winning is not the object in push hands; maintaining balance in relation to the other is.

Imagine you are standing in the "Tai Chi" itself—the so-called *yin-yang* diagram—with a foot in either spot. That's your universe; you should not go beyond it nor be pushed out of it. Another's energy, like the flow of the shapes within the diagram, changes endlessly from substantial to insubstantial in relation to your yielding and adherence. Your correct responses enable you to maintain balance within your "universe." But if another's energy grows excessive—too greedy or aggressive—your adherence and yielding should automatically result in his self-destruction. Justice.

Professor described this Confucian principle in Tai Chi Chuan as being a scale where weight on one end automatically produces an equal, opposite reaction on the other. Or think of a rake: step on the end and the handle comes up and hits you in the nose. Justice. The rake does not think in terms of right and wrong. The principle of balance produces the result.

Confucius and Lao Tzu were spoken of often and in depth, but there was another Chinese classic Professor occasionally mentioned.

In the 1960s the *I-Ching* developed into an icon of the counterculture. People were throwing coins and yarrow stalks, "consulting the oracle" about everything from their daily fortune to what to name their children. What did he think the first time I, with my beard and hippie ways, asked him about it?

He said, with his usual grin, "The *I-Ching* is the most profound classic of the Chinese sages. Confucius himself did not believe he was ready to *begin* the study of the *I-Ching* until he was 70."

"Can you give me any advice about how to use it?" As usual, I hadn't really heard him.

Patient with me as always, he said, "The most important words in using the *I-Ching* are Good/Not Good. Whatever the question—should I take a trip? Should I see this person? Good, not good?"

Not: What's going to happen, or what kind of year am

I going to have? You must at least take the effort to form the question: "Is it good or not good that I take this action?" And how much have you already accomplished by this effort?

Professor said that the principles of the *I-Ching* form the foundation for the teachings of Confucius, Lao Tzu and the entirety of Chinese culture.

23

Students of the Professor thought a lot about "getting it." "When am I going to get it—has he got it more than I?" The old man fostered this materialistic, non-Taoist attitude. A paradox of the Professor was that combined with his softness was an intensely competitive streak. He would make a competition out of anything. I recall him once sitting at his desk with a student who was a professional guitarist; they were pressing the tips of their fingernails together to see which would nick the other. A test of who had the most *ch'i* in his fingers. Needless to say who won.

Professor spoke of "getting it": "Encourage the best among you," he often said, "because if one of you gets it, he will bring you all along." Also, "I have about 60% of it; the very best students here have only 5%."

What was this "It" that we were supposed to be getting, and were so far away from?

In his *Thirteen Treatises* he described the three classic levels of development—Heaven, Earth and Human—and within the three main levels, nine degrees of development:

Human level:

    1. The technique of relaxing the ligaments from the shoulder to the wrist.

I can't tell for sure if he's holding a glass, but Professor often embarked upon a painting or work of calligraphy with a shot of whiskey.

For Professor, practicing calligraphy was the same as practicing the principles of Tai Chi: the whole body relaxed, moving as one piece, energy coming from the ground

One thing which always struck me about Professor was that he never had shoulder or upper-body tension in his gestures.

Professor fences with senior student Lou Kleinsmith. He loved to play with Lou. Professor told us we were too serious, that we should emulate Lou's sense of humor.

There were always some children running around the school.
Professor felt they really belonged there.

The school was a lively place, filled with Professor's personality and spirit. Intriguing activities, such as flower-arranging, were going on all the time.

Professor didn't speak English. Tam Gibbs was his translator, secretary, confidante. More than any of us, Tam was the classic disciple. His life was his relationship with Professor.

Ed Young was Professor's other translator. He put aside his
work as an artist during the years he assisted Professor.

In the last few years of his life, Professor spent more time on his study and teaching of the classics of Confucius and Lao Tsu. His lectures on these subjects were spirited and interesting.

Tam tries to push Professor, then he is gone. Trying to push Professor was like trying to find a ghost. Being pushed by him was like meeting the irresistible force.

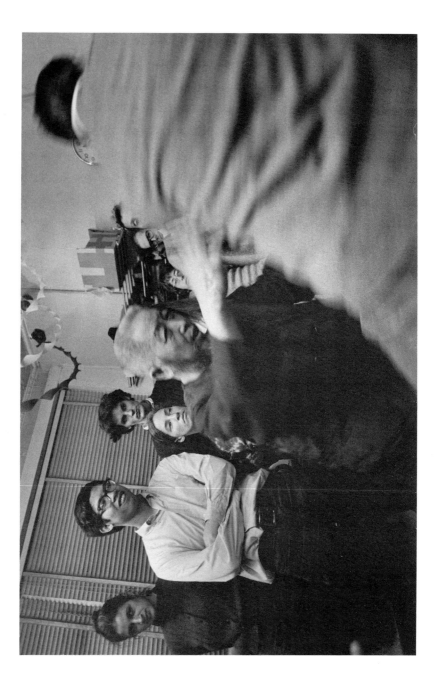

Professor explains a point about push-hands with Ken Van Sickle. Of all the arts, Professor said he liked teaching Tai Chi the best because it involved being with people.

Most of his time at the school was spent at this desk, where he would see patients, read pulses, then write herbal prescriptions in his notebook. Although he didn't speak English, he always communicated a great deal of concern and compassion.

Professor is doing the Tai Chi form. In his later years, it was unusual for students to see him doing the form in the school. On these rare occasions, the feeling of his form filled the room.

2. From the hip joint to the heel.
3. From the sacrum to the top of the head.

Earth level:

1. Sinking the *ch'i* to the *tan tien*.
2. The *ch'i* reaches the arms and legs.
3. The *ch'i* moves through the sacrum to the top of the head.

Heaven level:

1. Listening to or feeling strength.
2. Comprehension of *Chin* (internal power, the soft, pliable force used in Tai Chi Chuan).
3. Omnipotence level (the power without physical force).

The general implication was that if "It" was not an overtly martial quality, it definitely had to do with the power of Tai Chi Chuan. "The difference between yoga and Tai Chi," he once said, "is that even if you get it studying yoga, there's nothing you can do if someone tries to knock you off your cushion."

In addition to the classic stages of development, there are more mundane gradations—the way it works on the street, so to speak.

The average beginner is hard and insensitive. Normally he studies for less than a year, gets a taste of the art which can change his life, and has a valuable tool for health and relaxation. In "functional" terms, the martial application, he has nothing. If he tries to "use" what he knows of Tai Chi, he has less than nothing. He would be much better off running for his life, or picking up a chair in self-defense.

Interestingly, this is where the beginner and the master can be one, because if in a dangerous situation the beginner intuits the principle, he will not try to use Tai Chi to fight. Instead he will relax and "listen" to the heart of the situation;

in so doing he can often depolarize and completely defuse the threat. This experience, not uncommon, is often the inspiration that gives a beginner a deeper commitment to the art.

A major pitfall is that if the new student is not prepared to invest in loss, if he opts instead to start seeking victory, he runs the risk of being a perpetual beginner. Almost every school has its one or two students who have developed a modicum of sensitivity but, unwilling to further subdue their ego, desiring that Tai Chi pay off now, become demon push hands players, combining sensitivity with selective strength and resistance to push their opponents around. They have acquired techniques, they dominate any beginner and can be difficult for good players to handle, but all their victories are worthless. No matter how long they practice, the gate of real development has slammed shut; they have locked themselves out.

To avoid this it is important for the serious student to understand that his developing sensitivity tells him a great deal more about an opponent's stiffness than it does about his own. He cannot use techniques of softness—he must *become* soft, "the very atoms in his body must relax." Then his Tai Chi will start to work. This is not a process normally measured in years, it is measured in decades.

Having put in the time—or had an exceptional leap of understanding—the beginner becomes a Tai Chi player.

He has grown soft, and sensitive, not just toward another but toward himself as well. His upper body is loose and relaxed while his strength sinks down to his root, which has become very powerful.

He has learned about internal force, "the push in which the hands don't move," and correspondingly, he understands the double-weighting principle. He has reached the stage where double-weighting makes as much sense to him as walking in front of a moving truck. As a result, when his juniors push hands with him they are awed at how insubstantial he seems to be when they try to push him, and how substantial when he pushes them. When they try to release energy, they are amazed at how he seems to know what they're thinking before they do.

This serious student is most enthusiastic about his attainment at the times he is taken by surprise. Professor once said to his advanced students, "None of you know what you have until you have to use it."

Tam told a story of walking down a street in Chinatown when a friend came up from behind to surprise him with a slap on the back. Sensing the man's presence, Tam yielded to the slap, which caused his friend to lose his balance; he was about to fall when in one motion Tam reached out and caught the stunned fellow.

I've had a few similar experiences, most recently with the superintendent at the park where I practice in the mornings. The super, a strong, aggressive guy, grew curious about my strange exercise.

"But what would you do if someone came at you fast?"

"We only practice slow so that in a real situation we'll be able to move quickly," I answered, not completely confident.

He nodded; he was less than convinced.

Weeks later we were talking about the weather. Suddenly he shot a punch toward my belly. It was completely unexpected but I caught the punch before it landed. I don't know which of us was more surprised.

"Hey, you're really good," he said and held out his hand to congratulate me.

I put my hand in his but instead of giving me a handshake, he jerked my hand to pull me off balance.

My *gung fu* served me well. Instead of resisting, I went with his force so that he was unbalanced; at the same time

I pushed him. The combination of our two energies sent him more than 30 feet away. We were both impressed. "This Tai Chi stuff really works," he said.

The next day he presented me with a bouquet of flowers.

"Not knowing what you have until you have to use it" is the good news. The bad news for our advanced Tai Chi player is that when confronted, instead of being taken by surprise, he will probably stiffen up to some degree. Fear and ego will become involved and his Tai Chi will suffer.

His *gung fu* is more than skin-deep, but the *ch'i* hasn't sunk into his bones, nor has his psyche been transformed to where "a great mountain can collapse at his feet and his face would not change countenance."

This is where mastery lies. Who needs to worry about pushing or neutralizing when one's body is impervious to blows, when one's bones are like steel—when a powerful strike will only cause injury to the person striking? At the highest level we have "omnipotence," where as a result of one's spiritual development, an opponent can be thrown out with a look of the eye.

In *Zen In the Art of Archery*, Eugen Herrigel tells a story about the six years during which he studied traditional Japanese archery. He describes endless months of frustrating effort to develop to the point where the arrow falls from the bow like a leaf from a tree; where it is not he who is shooting the arrow—rather, "It" shoots.

"It" is what makes archery and Tai Chi spiritual disciplines. "It" is a manifestation of *Tao*.

From the end of my second through my seventh year of study, I was caught up in a Tai Chi dilemma, the mystery of the "push." How can you push without pushing? That's what Tai Chi principle asks you to do. You must be completely without strength from hand to shoulder. If not, you will shove, and a skillful opponent will detect and use your energy against you. "The correct push sprouts in the ground, springs from the legs, is directed by the waist, and only *emerges* from the hands," said Professor. "The secret of the push is that the hands should not move more than one inch, and they should not use more than four ounces of strength." It was ridiculous. He was asking us to push without pushing.

For five years I puzzled over this pushless push. I got to where I grew disgusted with my thousands of strong pushes. I could "hear" all the strength in my arms when I pushed, but when I let go of the strength and tried to push with my arms soft and loose—well, how can you push with limp spaghetti? As I said to my fellow Tai Chi bums, "It's like trying to milk a bull."

Others talked about the frustration of "investing in loss" when they were being pushed, the battering of the ego as they were bounced of the wall like a rubber ball. To me that was nothing compared to the frustration of "investing in loss" when you are trying to push without pushing.

"You're supposed to push me," my partner would complain, while I would stand there, with my two strands of limp spaghetti, my forehead bathed in sweat, hoping that through some divine intervention the internal energy would emerge from my hands like laser beams.

Bitterness? It is much more frustrating to invest in loss when you're supposed to win than when you're permitted to lose.

One day at the height of my frustration, when I had vowed never to use strength again until I discovered the secret, the old man asked me to play push hands. He put my hands on his wrist and elbow, smiled up at me and said, "Push."

I started sweating again. I knew endless years of what it was not; knew that I would shove at him with my arms and go flying while he laughed. I would not do it again.

But what could I do? He had said, "Push." I could not refuse. I knew a thousand times over what it was not: it was not shoving from the shoulder; it was not divine intervention. I could stand there for the rest of my life and the *ch'i* would not emerge from my arms like laser beams.

I knew very well what it was not; but what was it? Something to do with the body, I sensed. Not in the hands, but in the movement of the body. "The hands," he had said, "are like the bumper of a car. It is the car that moves, not the bumper."

So I leaned back and thrust my body forward. Not a thing came out of my hands, but our foreheads smacked together with a loud crack.

For an instant I feared I'd injured him. After a startled look, he laughed. "No, no," he pointed to his forehead, "Not here." He touched my hands to his wrist and elbow, "Here."

How do you push without pushing?

It went on for five years. I pondered the question not only while doing push hands but while walking, eating, sleeping. It was my koan, my mystery.

Then one day when Professor was in Taiwan, we were studying video tapes of him conducting a push hands class. I was watching him push and suddenly I saw it: It was so simple—everything he had said was true: "You don't push, the hands don't move, it's like the bumper of a car." Watching the video, I knew I could do it. When the lights went on afterward, I took a partner to the wall to test it out, but it was academic. I had come to understand it.

The understanding happened in an instant, but the five years were necessary. It's like drilling for oil; you have to get deep into the earth before the energy will flow forth. Not that it should take everyone as long. Before studying Tai Chi I had made a considerable investment in upper body strength;

I was as stiff and hard as a board. I had to undo every push-up I'd ever done.

The push comes from a combination of sensitivity and the power of the root; they come from the discipline of relaxation and nonaction.

I'm also afraid that for me the understanding was only the solution to my first koan, and not enlightenment. On more fundamental levels, I still use force. I haven't yet learned how to get out of the way and let "It" do it.

Studying with the old man gives one a different definition of "mastery" than is commonly understood, what with martial artist and spiritual "masters" on every street corner. It is more than flaws in technique that make the vast majority of those "masters" such gross self-deceivers. It's what you see in their eyes; they are caught up in fear and pride.

Liu Hsi Heng, whom Professor appointed to head his Taiwan school, is a man who in his 70s would never dream of calling himself "master." But he has a great deal of the old man's power and aura. He said he "got it" after Professor died.

There may be a clue here. A Zen saying has it that if you meet the Buddha, your response should be to "kill him." Holding on to the idea of a teacher or master ensures that they will do it for you, and that you are doomed to remain separate from "It." Perhaps ultimately we have had "It" all along, we just forget where we misplaced it.

24

Nothing in the world is more soft and weak than water
But for attacking the hard and strong
Nothing can surpass it.
And therefore nothing can take its place.
That the weak can overcome the strong
And the soft can overcome the hard
Is well known to the world
Yet no one can carry it out . . .

(Excerpt from *Tao Teh Ching*, Chapter 78,
from a lecture given by Professor Cheng)

The following is Professor Cheng's comment on the above chapter:

"This aspect of Lao Tzu, in which he talks about softness overcoming hardness, can be realized only through the practice of Tai Chi Chuan. A person who practices Tai Chi Chuan should use his intuition to understand the meaning of this idea.

"You need to feel the idea. When you push water, it will yield, but when it comes at you, it comes with its entire volume and you have no way of avoiding it. The power of water does not come by the drop or cup, it is the great volume that has the power.

"The *ch'i* in us is the same. One breath of *ch'i* is nothing, but when the *ch'i* has accumulated, it has the same power as a huge quantity of water. Consider this point carefully.

"Don't worry that you have no power. When you are

88

in contact with an opponent, and the force is coming at you, you have to yield. If you can yield and use *ch'i* to return the force, then you have power.

"There's an old Chinese saying: 'When a person pulls just one of your hairs, your whole body will follow him.' This is the sensitivity you need to develop; until you can make this understanding a part of yourself, you won't improve.

"When I push you, the power wells up from the root. There's no way for you to detect that it's coming, so you can't resist. If the force were only coming from the point of contact, the hands, the opponent would know you were coming and would not be there when you push.

"Water will not resist; if you push it, it will yield. If you can be like water, no one will be able to resist you, no matter how big and strong they are. This is the principle of Tai Chi boxing.

"If you are scared, though, the principle goes out the window. The only way to exercise the principle is to be without fear. If you are afraid of your opponent and he is not afraid of you, you might as well forget it.

"Water is not afraid. This is called 'the great fearlessness.' Only then can you be soft. On the other hand, if I am fearless but not soft, the principle won't work, either.

"First you must learn the principle, then cultivate it. Become soft and you will be less fearful, which will make you softer still, and then fearless. This is real, a person can achieve this."

25

I always resisted the old man. When I pushed hands with him, he bounced me off the wall like a yo-yo; my resistance made it possible. He would urge me to relax and be soft; but I held on to rigid body armor and willful tension like a drowning man clutching at a lifesaver.

I even resisted him before I met him. My friend David Blake and I were students at Thomas Boddie's uptown Karate dojo. Dave heard about Professor; at the time his name must have been resonating like distant thunder through the entire New York martial arts community. Dave went to see him and immediately gave up Karate to study Tai Chi Chuan.

Dave was a much better Karate player than I, and I respected his intelligence and sensitivity, but I stubbornly refused when he urged me to "visit and see what it's like."

Prior to studying Tai Chi, much of my life was motivated by a fear of being found out. I projected an image of toughness, but inside I felt like mush. Listening to Dave describe Tai Chi, I felt deeply threatened. I knew, with the wisdom of the heart, that what this Tai Chi stuff was about was letting go. For someone whose life was based on a defensive facade, "letting go" felt tantamount to self-destruction.

For six months Dave told me about Professor and Tai Chi. Finally I went down to see for myself.

When I walked through the door of the school, Professor was sitting at his desk in the front office. I have never seen such a thing before or since, but there was an aura around him at that moment—he was glowing golden.

I knew I had finally come home. Before I saw the form. Before I had experienced his awesome push hands. My heart—the sage within—knew that he was what I'd always dreamed of.

For many years I had lived with utter despair; my life felt like it was being spent in a dungeon. I'd desperately hoped that in some unknown way the door would open and I'd be let out into the light. Now here he was, the keeper of the keys.

"Most important is to relax," he said. "Let go of your tension and hard, stiff force. Open up all the passageways in your body to the flow of the *ch'i*." Leaving my first class as if I were floating on air, I said to myself, "This is as good as marijuana."

Marijuana was a serious drawback to progress—another area where I resisted the old man. I'd used it for all of my adult life, thinking it a lovely drug, gentle on the body and a valuable tool for the state of grace it led me to.

Professor had little patience with marijuana, dismissing it the one time I asked about it with, "It takes away from the kidneys." He was less harsh about other drugs. Alcohol was his drug of choice. He would also allow himself an occasional half-cup of coffee and generous amounts of lightly brewed tea. Though he didn't smoke, he said that a single cigarette after a meal was good for the digestion.

"Moderation in all things" was his watchword, but marijuana's effect of "taking away from the kidneys" was the kiss of death for him, making it all but poison. Of course, in his pharmacological philosophy, there is no poison that doesn't have some benefit and no "good" substance that won't be poisonous in excess. Marijuana, for example, hurts the kidneys but helps the stomach. I used to welcome an attack of diarrhea because I knew it was the one time Professor might approve of my marijuana smoking.

To the old man, "taking away from the kidneys" meant that marijuana injured the development of the *ch'i,* in which the kidneys play a central role. It has been only in the past few years, once I recognized my addiction and began abstaining, that I appreciate his warning.

The foundation of Tai Chi is in the legs; the kidneys relate to the strength of the legs. It is all but impossible to develop a deep root with even the occasional use of marijuana.

During all the years I smoked "moderately," once a week, I was aware of the price I was paying though I tried to repress the full implications. It felt to me like I was on a treadmill: drained on the weekend when I would smoke, gradually building my strength up during the week, only to deplete myself again the next weekend. Basically I was getting nowhere.

I didn't understand the deeper price I was paying. The power of *ch'i* provides the impetus for psychological as well as physical transformation. Marijuana represses fear and therefore provides a glimpse of *Tao,* the place of fearlessness and joy. But it puts the seeker on a spiritual and physical treadmill. The psychic batteries operating permanently at weak levels keep the seeker bouncing back and forth between depression and stimulated, low-level awareness.

Root fears are difficult to dissolve because they masquerade as other emotions: anger, jealousy, boredom, depression are all expressions of the deeper sense of self-abnegation and guilt most of us carry as permanent baggage. Addictions are so destructive to spiritual growth because they create fixation on surface problems rather than allowing one to deal with deeper issues.

Many beginning Tai Chi students come to their teacher saying: "I don't understand this Tai Chi. It's supposed to relax me, but I feel a lot more tense than when I started."

"Feel tense" are the key words. What is actually happening is that the student's body is coming alive; he is "hearing" his habitual stiffness and tension. For decades his shoulders had been up by his ears, "frozen there" as Professor would say. The student begins to relax, the stiffness begins to thaw out, so he can now sense what his body is really like. Logically, the initial feeling is not of improvement but of, "My God, my shoulders feel like they're up around my ears!"

It is hard to confront our real blockages. It is usually quite painful, which is why we need so much psychic and physical energy to persevere in the work.

In push hands, for instance, we yearn to tap into the flow of the *Tao* and let go of our fear because we feel essentially powerless in our lives. So we stop resisting and using force, and instead of being rewarded, the first thing that happens is we get pushed around. Constantly. By everyone.

This is difficult enough, but if we grow impatient and strive to gain victory over our opponents, we have the gnawing feeling that rather than tapping into the miraculous, we are just wasting our time being clever.

26

Professor said, "Tai Chi Chuan should be practiced without one's psychology influencing the physiology. If in push hands one's desire to push and fear of not being pushed take over, then it's no good. That's why Tai Chi is so difficult.

"If one does push hands like one does the exercise, it is correct. In addition, the four positions need to be practiced with a recognition of the truth, sincerity and integrity in yourself."

Is it possible to acquire the infinite sensitivity to the energy of Tai Chi Chuan if we indulge myriad insensitivities in the rest of our lives? Perhaps one of the greatest prices we pay for being macho creatures in a macho civilization is the way our sensitivity, like the blade of a fine sword, becomes dulled through the constant battering it takes.

A friend tells me she's going away. Refusing to admit my vulnerability, I deny the hurt in myself and turn a cold shoulder to her.

I walk down the street and pass a man I've seen hundreds of times practicing in the park with me. Out of fearful pride we pass without acknowledging that the other exists. Of course, it's true that we live in New York. Once, after my friend Jim Johnson and I had passed someone we recognized, without a nod, I commented that "In New York you don't say hello to someone unless you really know them."

"No," he disagreed, "In New York you don't say hello, especially if you know them."

Students becoming serious about Tai Chi practice notice its positive effect on their personality. Relaxation makes one less fearful, less prideful, more open to people and situations.

The cumulative effect of the "integrity" of the practice — integrity in the sense of "wholeness" — has the effect of moderating behavior, making one less prone to fly off the handle or go off the deep end. Integrity develops an individual's sense of responsibility, lessening the negative tendency to place blame on situations or other people.

27

Professor talked about the Taoist alchemy of Tai Chi Chuan much more than do the students who carry on his teaching, probably because what he had made real, development of his *ch'i*, is for us mainly theory. Our reticence is understandable, but to serve our fellow students and ourselves we have to bear in mind his emphasis on the "miraculous" in Tai Chi—his belief that it could be attained and that indeed it is the real purpose of the study.

The following excerpts are from a lecture on Taoism he gave in 1970 in which he encapsulated some of its principles.

"'*Sung*' means to relax, to be soft. Today, I'm going to talk about how you should work to become soft.

"The whole body has to give up its strength in order to relax.

"There are nine joints in the body that have to become loose: three in the arm, three in the leg and three in the back. The three in the arm are the wrist, elbow and shoulder. In the leg—hip, knee and ankle. In the back—sacrum, neck, top of the head.

"Of all the nine joints, the most important to work on are the three in the arm. First the wrist, then the elbow, then the shoulder. The shoulders are very hard to loosen.

"In order to loosen the joints, the first idea is that the tendons have to become loose, then the bones. You have to work on loosening the tendons between the joints. When the tendons are tight, the energy that comes out is angular, instead of with a natural flow. Because we have habits that are tight, we have to work at becoming loose.

"When we begin our study, our movements will be tight because of habit. We must learn to differentiate between action that is controlled by the heart/mind, and action that is not. Once the body has become loose, wherever the heart/mind focuses, the body will be free to follow.

"Of the three joints in the arm, the shoulder is the hardest to loosen. When the shoulder becomes loose, most of the problem is solved. Once the shoulder is loose, the other nine joints are much easier to loosen.

"The three joints in the leg depend on the three joints in the arm. Of the three joints in the leg, the ankle joint is the most difficult to loosen. When the person reaches the stage where he is working on loosening the ankle joint, he is almost there. Then he is ready to start on the back.

"When the sacrum joint is loosened, the *ch'i* starts up the back. Loosening the three joints of the back comes relatively late in training. Right now you should work on the three joints in the arm. When the shoulder is loosened, I'll talk about the other joints.

"Once you become loose, you have to work on the *ch'i*. The exercising of the *ch'i* is very different from Western-style exercises.

"There are three kinds of *ch'i*: the *ch'i* of the air, the *ch'i* of the blood, and the *ching ch'i*, the essence of the internal organs. When the *ching ch'i* becomes full it becomes the spiritual aspect of the person.

"To work on the three kinds of *ch'i*, bring the *ch'i* of the

97

air into the *tan tien*. Focusing your heart/mind on the *tan tien* will allow the *ch'i* of the air to eventually accumulate and have effect.

"There are four words to bear in mind when thinking about the air going into the *tan tien*: the breath should be thin, long, quiet and slow. It is like drawing the silk from a cocoon. Of these four words we start with the last, the slowness. By being slow, the breath becomes thin and delicate, then it becomes long and the quietness follows.

"It is *not* forcing the air down. It is keeping the heart/mind focused on the *tan tien* that leads the air there. As far as breathing is concerned, it is not a conscious act.

"When the idea is in the *tan tien*, then gradually everything will work its way down. Once the *ch'i* accumulates in the *tan tien*, the person will gain marvelous benefit without knowing ahead of time what the benefits will be. Five thousand years ago when the Yellow Emperor said, 'Swallow the *ch'i* of heaven to reach the godhead,' these were not empty words.

"*Ch'i* is in everything that is alive. If it doesn't have *ch'i*, it is no longer alive, it will wilt. In Tai Chi Chuan we want to begin with the *ch'i*.

"We start with the hands. There is a point in the center of the hand called 'the laborious palace'; after *tan tien* awareness, this is the beginning of your awareness of the *ch'i*. Since this point in the hand is hollow, the strength of the hand cannot reach there, but the *ch'i* can. When the *ch'i* of the hand reaches there, the arm has become loose.

"The next point is the 'Rushing Spring,' the Taoist name for the point in the feet where the root connects with the ground. The last point is the hole in the top of the head. These five points cannot be reached by strength, but the *ch'i* can reach there. Gradually you will feel these five points. Start by concentrating in the *tan tien*, then allow the *ch'i* to reach these five points.

"Coming to understand the value of Tai Chi Chuan, the practitioner will become persistent. When a person studies Tai Chi Chuan hoping to understand it quickly, he will not be able to get it.

"The *I-Ching* says: 'The movement of the sky is constant, humanity exists because of it. The sage fashions his life according to the constancy of heavenly bodies.'

"This implies that a person becomes powerful by constant activity which improves his health. A person who goes without rest is in contrast to a society that rests two days out of seven. The body can rest, but the mind, the spirit, has to go on, even if the body is at rest. Otherwise it would be like the heavenly bodies resting two days out of seven.

"The idea of the spirit not resting relates to the *ch'i*; it must keep going. The heart/mind should be kept in the *tan tien* without a moment's rest. This is exercising the *ch'i* constantly, like the movement of the heavens.

"To understand this idea is to make a decision to study Tai Chi Chuan. These words are important. If you follow them, you won't regret it."

Later Professor addressed the apparent harshness of the idea, "exercise the *ch'i* constantly, without a moment's rest." He told a story of Confucious walking in the company of his disciples.

"Master," said a disciple, "how is it possible to follow *Tao* constantly, without resting?"

Confucius pointed to a graveyard that they happened to be passing. "Don't worry about resting," Confucius said. "Later on you will have plenty of time for that."

Professor's main techniques for the critical work of loosening the joints of the arm were the "beautiful lady's hand" and "the hanging elbow."

The wrist should be gently rounded instead of angular and stiff, allowing the *ch'i* to flow to the fingertips. If there is tension or hard force, the wrist will be stiff and "broken" — not gently rounded. The "beautiful lady's hand" is an epitome of Non-Action, because any idea of "doing" — manipulating, forcing or blocking — will cause the wrist to be tense and angular. In order to do Tai Chi, the wrist and hand must be channels of internal energy, with no addition of force. The "beautiful lady's hand" is the first gate of the *ch'i*. While progress through the "nine gates" is not strictly linear, one must achieve the idea of "beautiful lady's hand" as the first step on the path of Tai Chi Chuan.

The second gate is the "hanging elbow." Thinking of the elbow as hanging and weighted empties the critical shoulder joint of force and tension. When using hard, external energy the hand is heavy and the elbow light. Soft, internal energy is the reverse — light hand, heavy elbow. It is only through persistent, diligent application that the first two gates open, allowing the critical shoulder joint to open; and it is only at that point that one becomes a Tai Chi boxer.

28

One day a student announced that he wanted to ask about the relationship of sexual practices and Tai Chi.

Lou said, "Take my advice, don't ask. You're not going to like the answer."

The fellow did not heed the warning. When the question was translated Professor said, "This question is very important. I want to give a little talk about it."

As we left the office for the main room, Lou repeated. "I warned you, you're going to be sorry."

Professor began:

"In Chapter III of the *Tao Teh Ching*, Lao Tzu says 'The Sage's way of governing is by relaxing the mind, reinforcing the abdomen, softening the will, strengthening the bones.'

"Lao Tzu is trying to express the advantages of Non-Action. That is why he says the Sage governs by relaxing the mind, meaning that the mind is completely at rest to the extent that no action is even contemplated.

"'Reinforcing the abdomen' does not mean to fill the stomach with food, as many other commentators have interpreted. It means to fill the *tan tien* with *ch'i*. Just as the Yellow Emperor said, 'The Sage swallows the *ch'i* of heaven to reach spiritual enlightenment.'

"'Weakening the will' has to do with the fact that the will is stored in the spleen. The idea corresponds to 'strengthening the bones,' which belong to the kidneys. 'The kidneys' actually means the entire uro-genital system. The kidneys are the root of life before birth and govern the primal energy. The spleen is the root of life after birth. If the will—from the spleen—is too strong, it will not only damage the primal energy, it will also destroy the root of life.

"So how do we strengthen the bones? For the male it is done by nourishing an element in the semen called *ching* and filling the bones with a special marrow, as was stated by Chi Po, the teacher of the Yellow Emperor: 'Marrow and bones becoming strong is the foundation of life.'

"This is the most important chapter in Lao Tzu. It is often misinterpreted because most commentators do not understand Chinese medical theory and practice.

"Chinese medicine puts great emphasis on the development of the *ch'i*. The *ch'i* circulates like blood, and the *tan tien* is the seat of the *ch'i*. The *tan tien* is located one and three-tenths inches below the naval; three-tenths from the front of the body, seven-tenths from the back.

"The *ch'i* accumulates from the *tan tien* by means of blood vessels, membranes, the space between membranes and the tendons. Circulating through the body, the *ch'i* pulls the blood like a horse pulls a chariot.

"A cornerstone of Chinese philosophy is the 'Five Elements' theory. It establishes that the material world is made up of five elements—metal, water, wood, fire and earth—which interact with one another in creative or destructive ways: Metal creates water and destroys wood; water creates wood and destroys fire; wood creates fire and destroys earth; fire creates earth and destroys metal; earth creates metal and destroys water.

"Chinese medicine joins philosophy, with the five elements corresponding to the five organs of the body. The heart, lungs, spleen, kidneys and liver correspond to the five elements:

"The lungs correspond to metal; kidneys to water; liver to wood; heart to fire; spleen to earth. Where the five elements create or destroy one another, in Chinese medical theory the five organs also help or hurt one another.

"Each organ has an emotion connected to it. The will is the emotion connected to the spleen. So when Lao Tzu says "subdue the will," he is referring to medical theory in which the will and spleen, becoming too strong, damage the kidneys, as earth destroys water.

"When he says, 'Strengthen the bones,' he is talking about the process of accumulating *ch'i* in the *tan tien*, creating a special, miraculous kind of *ch'i*.

"A man begins this process with seminal fluid created in the uro-genital system. This fluid goes to the *tan tien* where it joins with the *ch'i* of the blood, directed to the *tan tien* by the will. Then you breathe in the *ch'i* of heaven and direct it to the *tan tien*. The seminal *ch'i*, called *ching ch'i*, gathers in the *tan tien* with the *ch'i* of the blood and the *ch'i* of the heavens. Staying there long enough, they will come to generate a kind of steam, something like electricity. This steam flows out of the *tan tien*, through the sacrum and into the spine and bones, where it condenses into a paper-thin tissue. This type of marrow gradually fills the bones, causing them to become hard like steel. Then it flows up the spine to the brain and finally returns to the *tan tien*.

"You should pay special attention to the Yellow Emperor's words, 'The Sage swallows the *ch'i* of heaven to achieve spiritual enlightenment.' This is also the process whereby a sage can sit alone in his room and come to know everything.

"It is necessary for a man to conserve the *ching*, the element in the semen that gathers in the *tan tien*. Ejaculation depletes the *ching*. For a 16-year-old man, it takes the *ching* seven days to replenish itself after ejaculation. For a man of 24, it takes two weeks to replenish itself; for a man of 32, it takes three weeks; and for a man of 40 it takes 40 days. Once you reach 50, you should hold onto your *ching* for life. You have the potential of having 120 years of life. Depleting your *ching* is like taking money out of your bank account: you lose days of your life every time."

This talk unleashed a firestorm of interest. In the following weeks Professor Cheng elaborated to an extent, but the disturbing issue of the *ching ch'i* was left hanging. On one point at least, it was obvious he did not practice what he preached. He had fathered children in his 50s, ignoring his own warning that after 50 "you should hold onto your *ching* for life."

Professor explained that a man could either live celibately like a Taoist hermit, conserving *ching* for spiritual development, or he could go out into the world. Secular life involved compromises with spiritual ambition, one such compromise being the imperatives of procreation. Stated another way, a man chooses to create himself or create the world. As for the basis of his own "choice," Professor often said that his desire was not to become a living Buddha, just to become a human being.

For some of us life became a good deal more complicated after he introduced the concept of the *ching ch'i*.

"Is there an art of having orgasms without ejaculating?" an enterprising fellow asked.

"Yes, there is, but in China only bad people do this — men who wish to exercise power over women."

One implication of cultivating the *ching ch'i* is that sex and ejaculation need not be synonymous. The man who sees ejaculation as the lone focus of love-making drastically limits the quality of his sexual activity.

"Downward drained" is the Chinese term to describe a man who indulges in excessive ejaculation. The condition is like an addiction: the more drained one becomes, the greater the compulsion to drain further. "Downward draining" can injure the health and even result in death. Very different from the prevalent Western theory, "Use it or lose it."

Professor explained that this is one more area where women have a natural advantage over men. A woman's *ching ch'i* is present in the blood rather than the semen. In women the *tan tien* is located just above the womb, and the *ching* is egg-producing.

Though women don't have the problem of depleting the *ching* through ejaculation, Professor said a woman pays a different price for immoderate sexual behavior. Since the years when she can have children are much more limited than the male's, a woman sacrifices the opportunity to have children if she chooses to "play around" during her fertile years.

29

"In revering the teacher you will not only benefit from his teaching, you actually can become harmonised with his knowledge. If you neither revere your teacher nor give consideration to those without understanding, to whom you are an example, you are indeed confused. To know this is an essential tenet of the Tao."—From an oral commentary professor gave on Lao Tzu's Chapter 27

Liu Hsi-heng, Professor's successor in Taiwan, said that a teacher should not only work with you on the art of Tai Chi Chuan, but on becoming truly human and behaving properly:

"The principles of Tai Chi Chuan can be used totally in the living of life. For instance, in Tai Chi Chuan we put importance on yielding, on how to invest in loss. We must learn to be tender, soft and peaceful. These are also the principles of how to cultivate your mind and get along with others smoothly."

It was a relief to finally meet Mister Liu. Having studied with Professor, I have a very different sense of the word "master" than the way it is generally used. The primary difference between Professor and the 10,000 little masters is not between his transcendent ability and their vast limitations; more it is in the quality of his person. Perhaps the word "harmonious" best expresses it.

Over the years, a doubt began to grow in my mind: it was not the principles of the art he espoused but some accident of the genes, an evolutionary mutation, which produced the old man. No matter how hard we studied, I feared that the rest of us were doomed to fall short of the mark.

Liu Hsi-heng was in his 70s when I met him, and more than his ability, it was his character that put my gnawing doubts to rest. Another old guy had it, had become sweet, fearless and harmonious. He attributed it to his teacher and to the study of Tai Chi Chuan.

I took a workshop with Mister Liu. At the end of two days during which he worked much harder than anyone else, he was still full of energy and enthusiasm. Past the time when the workshop was supposed to end, he was still on his feet, eagerly answering questions.

The Professor also had fantastic energy. It has to do, I believe, with personal clarity. Our fears and defenses drain the *ch'i* and sap energy. Heightened vitality and happiness are the rewards for clearing out the negative.

When I did push hands with Mr. Liu I remembered what I hadn't experienced since Professor died. It is the paradox of Tai Chi done well that it is an unsurpassed yet also nonviolent martial art.

Getting pushed is generally no fun. We are at best defeated and frustrated, at worst humiliated or hurt.

The correct push, however, is done with Non-Action. Mr. Liu didn't push me, I pushed myself, or more exactly my resistance and the principle operating through him resulted in my being pushed.

When someone is pushed according to the Tai Chi principle, there are no negative feelings. You don't feel the pusher's will operating against you; your ego doesn't react. It is like taking a ride in an amusement park—shocking but fun. Tai

Chi points to a theoretical condition where a fight can be won without destroying the harmony of the winner or loser. On the deepest level the principle is non-violent, caring and compassionate toward the other as it is toward the self.

Mr. Liu says, "The first thing you have to learn is the spirit of it's better to give over than to try to get; or it's better to extend rather than hoping others will extend to you. This involves a spirit of sacrifice; in a larger sense it is to become a person of 'no-self,' or to lose the self, in everything you do. You do not think of yourself, but of the society, the country and the world."

30

"Do push hands as if no one is there, do the form as if someone is there." — Professor Cheng

Martial ability in Tai Chi develops through osmosis. Correct and, as Professor would say, "sincere" practice of the form and push hands produces a body wisdom, an instinctual power that when initially emergent surprises the practitioner.

Practicing with the goal of achieving martial proficiency has the opposite result. The student remains hard and tense and whatever fighting skill he demonstrates is a manifestation of the aggressiveness, speed and strength he brought to the study. It is not to be spoken of in the same breath as Tai Chi Chuan.

The student must become completely soft for the process of osmosis to take effect; then the student becomes a Tai Chi boxer. She must push hands as if no one were there. Few are capable of putting this idea into practice because it is hard to literally accept. Most students harbor the notion that not using force or resistance is a metaphor, a measure of the spirit of the thing rather than a literal statement of method.

But a real Tai Chi boxer is like a ghost — try to push her and she is not there, while her own power is irresistible. To manifest this, you must practice as if you were a ghost. The opponent's energy comes at you and you cannot resist — no more than four ounces of pressure should build up — you must not be there. If this means you get pushed over – as it almost certainly will for your early years – you will ride with the force but you will lose nothing but empty pride. If you are diligent your softness will become second nature, and you will have transformed yourself. The opponent will never experience your resistance or feel your force on his body; only its result will be apparent as he goes flying. And he will be unable to focus his strength on you, either through attack or resistance. You will come to know the method and wonder of doing push hands "as if no one is there."

Doing the form as if someone *were* there relates more directly to the fighting aspect of Tai Chi Chuan.

In the initial stage, the entire focus of the practice should be on eliminating all tension and hard force. In this stage any specific martial ideas – that this or that movement is for the purpose of breaking an elbow or bursting a kidney – would only produce physical hardness.

Once the student has become soft and begun to experience *ch'i* in his play, he is ready to have his focus be other than just letting go of tension. He must begin to do the form as if someone were there. Not with hard, stiff force, but with the tool he has begun to develop, the power of the *ch'i*. He must practice with the image – Professor's word was the "idea" – of focusing the massed, integrated power of his *ch'i* in every posture.

This is not trivial. The softness and sensitivity the student is acquiring appear inconsistent with deadly martial applications. Many students shy away from confronting the issue. Some remain hard and keep themselves from having to experience the fierce power of *ch'i*; others repress it by turning softness into an unfocused dance.

How does using one's heart/mind to visualize the idea of inflicting fatal harm fit in with learning the *Tao* of softness, the ability to harmonize, to become sensitive, gentle and tender?

It is a paradox that real softness can only come from strength. If the essence of the person is weak and fearful, he may put on a gentle act, but the reality he manifests is hard. A person compensates for internal weakness by becoming aggressive and defensive.

A transformation is required, one that cannot occur when a person sees Tai Chi as an empty dance or a shoving match.

When a person relaxes his physical tension and psychological brittleness, allowing *ch'i* and self-acceptance to take their place, he grows soft and powerful.

Human beings have been civilized for a tiny fraction of the history of the species. Beneath the suits and dresses are primal genes. Even if it is never acted out, the potential for violence is at the core of the games people play, a kind of hidden text. Arrogant people employ it as a threat, timid people fear to confront it. Both conditions are out of balance and create trouble. Martial ability enables one to understand and come to terms with the subtextural violence, both in oneself and in others. It enables the practitioner to soften his hard edges and defuse or deflect the aggression of others. The deeper your *gung fu*, the less likelihood you will have to use it. Arrogance and fear draw trouble, internal power and centeredness bring forth wellbeing.

31

In addition to Tai Chi Chuan, Professor taught an extensive system of massages and techniques for maintaining good health through nurturing the *ch'i*.

These massages are self-directed, not massaging another person. Basic to all of them is that they be done without muscular force. It is the "idea" directing the *ch'i* that is doing the massage, and the idea comes from the heart, not the brain. The hands exert only the gentlest pressure, just a light touch to guide the *ch'i*.

KIDNEY MASSAGE

The most important massage is for the kidneys, or actually the urogenital system which is governed by the kidneys. The urogenital system relates to the nurturing and development of the *ch'i*, as well as to the strength of the legs.

Use the backs of the wrists to rub gently up and down from the outside of the lower back to the base of the spine, the angle of the massage forming a V-shape. Forty-nine strokes up and down constitute a complete massage. Professor said that if you do one additional stroke make that be the start of another complete 49. This is the only massage Professor said everyone should do once a day. The other massages are done to suit particular circumstances.

Professor specified the number of strokes for each massage, the number varying from massage to massage. I can't explain the numbers, but I have come to understand a reason for counting: the massages are done with the heart/mind. You cannot do that while talking or watching T.V. You must concentrate. Counting directs the mind to the job at hand.

FINGER MASSAGE

Using the fingertips of the massaging hand, draw the *ch'i* out from the wrist to the end of the thumb, index and middle fingers. Then, reversing the direction, use the fingertips to send the *ch'i* back from the ends of the ring and pinky fingers to the wrist. To repeat: draw the ch'i out with the first three fingers, send it back on the last two. Massage all ten fingers twenty-one times in succession.

The fingers can be thought of like the nozzle of a garden hose, the entire body being the rest of the hose. Having the *ch'i* flowing in the fingertips is like the water flowing out of the nozzle of a hose—it is a sure indication that the water, or *ch'i*, is circulating through the rest of the hose. This massage is not only beneficial for the hands and circulatory problems like arthritis, but it is good for the entire body.

The *ch'i* has a central role in circulation. Professor said that the *ch'i* pulls the blood like a horse pulls a chariot; where the *ch'i* goes, the blood will follow.

A not incidental benefit of this massage is the effect it has on headaches. It has little effect on headaches caused by indigestion but is marvelously curative for tension headaches.

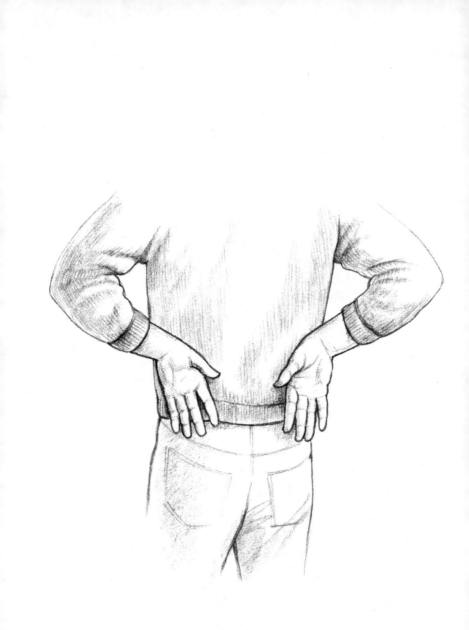

The Kidney Massage

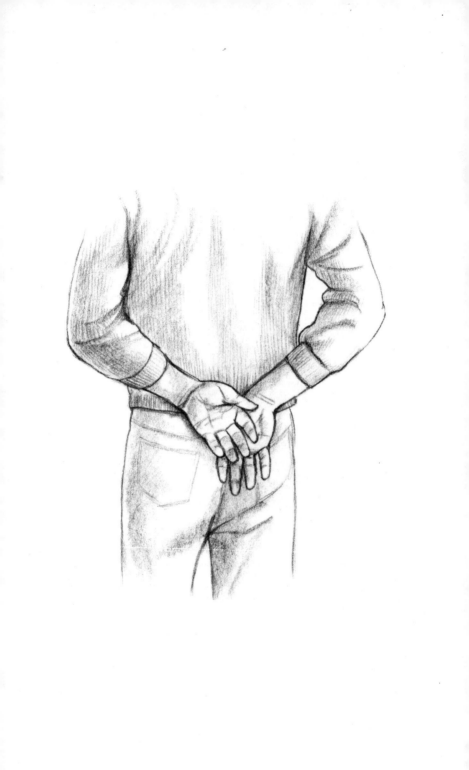

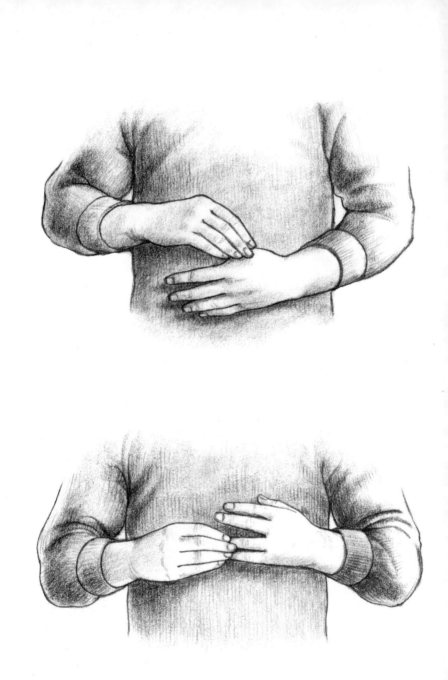

The Finger Massage

EYE MASSAGE

Place the index finger of each hand above the eyebrows. Close the eyes. Using the first knuckle of the thumb, massage the inner plane of the socket, above and below each eye. Start near the nose and circle down and around to the outer edge of the eye socket, then up and around the top half of the socket back to the nose, completing the circle. Do it 36 times.

It is good for sight, as well as relief of irritation, and even getting rid of a foreign object in the eye.

This massage has been particularly beneficial to me. Probably because of a number of years in which I worked as a word processor, I developed nearsightedness and took to wearing glasses. One day Professor told me that if I wanted to work on the problem, I could cure my bad vision. Following his advice, the first thing I did was throw away my glasses. Then, using the eye massage as the foundation, I began to re-train my eyes, dissolving the tension which had affected my vision. I had a difficult few months in which movies and television were a blur, but within a year my eyesight was as good as new.

A lot of vision trouble comes from tension. The massage gives the message "relax" to the eye, and if tension is the problem, the vision improves immediately. It also imparts a subtle lesson: "If you can just stop trying so hard, relax and let the vision come to you, you will see fine. The problem is that you have lost faith in your sight so you have been anxiously trying to grab the objects you want to see." Eyestrain is a kind of force, a kind of tension, and everything works better without force and tension.

This quality of receptivity, of just allowing things in, an aspect of the Non-Action we study in Tai Chi, benefits all the senses. Not forcing, not *trying* to hear, lets you hear better.

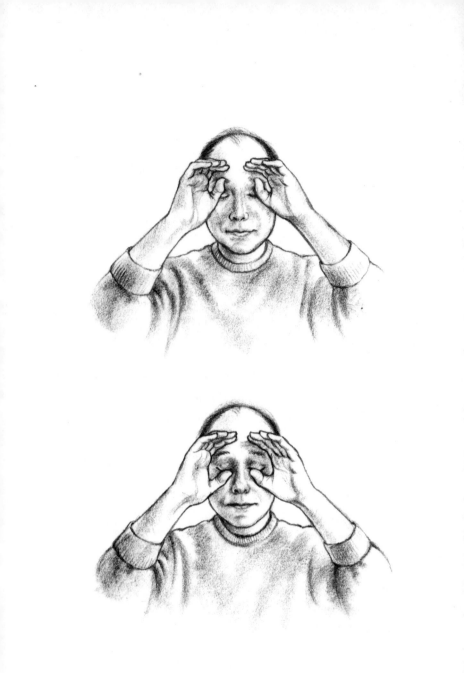

The Eye Massage

Relaxing the voice improves its quality, as any good singer knows. The secret is having faith, giving up the feeling that we need to use force to make things happen, and relaxing.

FOOT MASSAGE

Using the center of the palm, stroke it over the center of the foot (the "Rushing Spring") from the heel to the toes. Forty-nine strokes for each foot. A good time for this massage is right before bed. In case of a cold Professor recommended rubbing salt on the soles of the feet. Then put socks on for the night to sweat out the cold.

NECK MASSAGE

Using the center and heel of the palms, rub from the base of the neck up the back of the neck and skull. It is more effective than twisting the head and neck.

BELLY MASSAGES

To relieve discomfort caused by over-eating and to aid digestion, rotate the right hand from the outside to the inside edge as you run the palm down from the chest to the belly button.

To reduce the size of the belly and loosen the waist: Circle the fist around the *tan tien* 36 times. Turn the waist to go in the direction of the fist, as if playing push hands with oneself. Professor was fond of this massage and did it often, though as Bob Smith has noted, with little apparent effect on his persistent pot belly.

These are the primary massages, but one of Professor's basic thoughts for good health was (1) do Tai Chi Chuan and (2) if it hurts, rub it. Rubbing aids the circulation of the *ch'i*, and the presence of the *ch'i* is beneficial for any physical malady.

If suffering from a serious blow, rub and accompany the rubbing with jumping up and down to prevent the *ch'i* from getting stuck in the body.

In addition to the massages, Professor taught many other techniques and procedures for good health. Here are a few:

"Chew your drink and drink your food" was an aspect of Professor's dictum, "Don't eat too much or too fast. The weapons we have most to fear are the knife and fork." "Chewing your drink" guards against gulping; "drinking food" means that you chew enough to make food easily digestible.

Professor warned against food or drink that is too hot or cold. "Ice cold" is a special problem in modern civilization. "You might as well take poison as eat or drink something that is ice cold," he said.

Upon waking in the morning, do the form "before performing your morning ablutions." Should you need to urinate right after waking up, have a drink first; have a bit of food before defecating. If you do your form first, you don't need to eat or drink before going to the toilet. As to the ablutions: wash your head in the morning and your feet at night.

For bruises, sore muscles, sprains: the very first thing upon waking in the morning, take the first morning saliva on your fingers and rub it on the sore or injured place. Professor said that the saliva just after you awake has special healing properties. It corresponds to the dew on plants: "Take dew off plants and they die."

Often he would prescribe liquor for medicinal purposes. I was especially fond of his "two hats cure." In case of a cold, goes the prescription, go home and put your hat on the bedpost. Then get a bottle of scotch and start drinking. When you've drunk enough to see two hats on your bedpost, get into bed, pull up the covers and sweat out the cold. Whether or not it works, it can sure make having a cold more fun.

Scotch for colds but brandy for stomach disorders. Diarrhea especially seems to respond to a couple of ounces.

Professor said that in general liquor has a positive effect on the circulation of the *ch'i*. Liquor helps one relax and represses fear—the reason most people drink. Both aid the *ch'i*. Additionally, a drunk is loose and weighted, primary principles of Tai Chi Chuan. As a result, a drunk is less prone to injury from blows or falls, and his own force is heightened as anyone knows who has had to deal with one.

It is equally true that drunks often get injured and are not very good fighters. According to Professor, the crucial difference between a drunk and a Tai Chi boxer is the "idea," the presence and expression of the heart/mind: subtle, open, centered and vital. All the things a drunk's mind is not.

The Tai Chi form itself can be thought of as a series of massages, remedies and preventatives for physical maladies. The postures relate to specific areas of the body: for example, "Cloud Hands" for neck and back trouble. Professor said that Cloud Hands derives from the animal posture called The Bear. "Bears have strong backs," Professor said. "If you watch bears in the zoo, you will see them swaying back and forth in an attitude reminiscent of Cloud Hands."

With The Bear in mind, Professor taught a 49-repetition, swaying-back-and-forth movement to strengthen the back. The feet are placed at about twice shoulder width. As in Cloud Hands, you shift the weight and turn the waist from side to side. The arms are loose and swing with the weight shift and waist turn. For additional benefit, allow your hands to flow with the momentum and lightly tap the kidney area with each swing.

The pigeon-toed postures of the form are also good for the lower back; so too is Repulse Monkey.

Professor said that the most important posture for health

is Single Whip: "It is the great opening posture." The Single Whip is of special value in dealing with weakness of the lungs. That Tai Chi cured him of his "terminal" case of tuberculosis probably heightened Professor's appreciation of this posture. He also recommended repetitions of Squatting Single Whip for relief from the discomfort of over-eating.

Moderation is a central theme in Professor's philosophy of good health. Don't over-eat, "Leave the table a little hungry." Don't sleep too much, "Owe yourself a little sleep." Even exercise can be injurious if it is overdone. Speech and laughter should not be extreme in pitch or volume.

He warned against extremes in diet. He thought electric juicers were a problem because they made it possible to consume excessive quantities of the *ch'i* of a particular food that you would not be likely to consume if you had to work through the process of chewing and swallowing. He did not agree with the principle of macrobiotics. "These macrobiotic diets will kill you," he said as he examined a wan young adherent.

He advised that we not seek out exotic foods. "Best is to eat those foods that are indigenous to the region where you are living. They contain the qualities of nourishment that a person in that area requires for good health."

The emotions should not be extreme: "Too much anger hurts the liver; excessive grief injures the lungs; extreme fear hurts the kidneys."

The art is to find balance in all things. "There is no poison that cannot aid health in the right circumstance and no 'virtuous substance' that will not be poisonous in excess." Physical or psychological well-being requires moderation. Whether it is the health of the individual, nation or planet, if the balance is upset, misfortune will result.

32

The study of Tai Chi is a commitment to being present, the very opposite of tuned-out, addictive behavior. It becomes increasingly difficult to lie to oneself or escape reality if one is practicing sensitivity and balance. Additionally, there are specific qualities of the discipline of Tai Chi conducive to learning how to face life rather than run away from it.

One of the first ideas a beginner works on is to move as one piece, with torso, shoulders and head all moving from the waist, "the nose in line with the belly button." The relaxed gaze is aligned with the center, not wandering about or looking forward in anticipation of where we're going. It is an excellent antidote for the tendency to skitter away from life by perpetually looking back at the past or toward the future. The vital "now" is real; all other time is illusion, and dwelling in it robs life of its spark.

The quality of walking in Tai Chi Chuan is centered and quite different from the way most people move. The method is to "place down an empty foot, like a cat walking." This is in contrast to the common tendency to place weight in the stepping foot. There are fundamental benefits of this "empty foot," cat-like movement. Since there is no weight in the foot, should it meet an unexpected obstacle it can be instantly withdrawn. Because of the weight in the foot in normal stepping, once the foot goes forward it is committed—and tripping is the result of its meeting an unseen or unexpected obstacle.

As the practitioner incorporates the quality of Tai Chi movement into his life, he finds that he stops banging into things. The result of not falling into each step provides the opportunity to instantaneously ease back from unexpected barriers.

Tai Chi movement comes from being balanced and rooted in the non-stepping foot, rather than falling from step to step. This leads to much greater stability and alertness, a reason why it is so hard to take a good Tai Chi player by surprise, as well as why the practitioner can be so relaxed.

The quality of cat-like alertness, called *ling*, should be the state of the Tai Chi practitioner when he is standing still, sitting or resting. When standing, the weight should be primarily on one leg rather than evenly distributed on both legs. With weight on one leg, movement can be instantaneous. Weight on both legs—double-weighting—is stagnant, not *ling*.

Professor was once sitting and drinking tea, talking with a friend, when another old-timer crept up behind him to test his *gung fu* with a playful shove in the back. Professor instantly gave way before the shove, and meeting no resistance, it was the old-timer who was taken by surprise, stumbling past the Professor and almost falling. The Professor did not spill a drop of tea.

He taught that sitting in a chair one should be alive, not stagnant. The method is in maintaining the quality of rootedness, feet suporting the weight, even though one is sitting. "The back of the chair is for hanging your coat," Professor said. In other words, you should not lean back in the chair, losing your *ling*.

124

Sit balanced on the edge of the chair. "If you are really tired," he said, "don't slump in a chair. Lie down and go to sleep."

It should be noted that even sleep need not rob a Tai Chi practitioner of his *ling*. Professor told a story of being in Taiwan on a very hot, humid night. Mrs. Cheng, their newborn child and the Professor moved out of the bedroom, put a mattress down on the living room floor where it was cooler, and went to sleep. In the middle of the night Professor suddenly found himself sitting upright, supporting with great effort a heavy metal plaque which had somehow fallen off the mantelpiece and would've landed on his wife and child had he not caught it.

The story reeked of the magical until a number of years later, on two occasions, I found myself suddenly awake out of a deep sleep, having caught a heavy blow aimed at me by my sleeping companion—obviously a much longer story in itself—with absolutely no clue as to what had awakened me in that split second.

The Tai Chi Classics and other writing on Tai Chi make frequent references to the cat-like quality of Tai Chi. People whose minds have been conditioned to jump about from past to future, who feel bored or anxious doing less than 20 different things at the same time, judge the quality of the cat's relaxed focus in the present as stupidity. I had a similar feeling when I first started studying the old man doing push hands. He had a strange quality of non-anticipation, relative to those with whom he would play. You could see his partner's mind racing, "What will happen if I do this? What about that tactic?" Chatter, chatter, chatter. Professor would be at rest in the present, looking stupid to my mind, with no apparent thought or preconception, just patiently awaiting whatever happened next, like a cat waiting to catch a bird.

Ling refers to this quality of aliveness which is the essence of Tai Chi practice. The *ch'i* is the basis of life, the mysterious "it" that precedes circulation and all the rest of the body's mobile chemistry and electricity. The absence of *ch'i* is death. It is the basis of Professor's statement, "Softness is the *gung fu* of life, hardness is the *gung fu* of death." Where there is softness, the *ch'i* can flow so that the organism — be it person or planet — is alive. Hardness is rigidity, the absence of flow; the *ch'i* is gone, the result is death. In English, the colloquialism for a dead body is "a stiff."

33

Professor did not teach supplementary *Ch'i Kung* exercises because the core of his Tai Chi is *Ch'i Kung*. ("*Ch'i Kung*": the discipline of nurturing and developing the *ch'i*.) Everything about our Tai Chi is rooted in its relevance to the nurturing and developing of the *ch'i*.

Professor did not teach things that could not be felt and touched. If our heads are connected to heaven, our feet must still be firmly rooted in the earth. He warned us, for instance, that if we felt the need to supplement our Tai Chi with sitting meditation, "Beware of having visions. It is an indication that you're off the track and can be dangerous to your health." The recommended supplementary meditation was to sit cross-legged on the floor, or in a chair with your feet on the ground. "In olden days when people sat in lotus position on the floor, it was much healthier," he said, "because of the benefit of sitting with the feet close to the *tan tien*. However, the lotus position is too hard if you haven't practiced it, so sitting in a chair is OK." One should sit relaxed and straight, with the hands folded in the lap, the thumb of the left hand touching the middle finger and the thumb of the right hand placed through the circle of the left hand's thumb and middle finger, and resting against the last joint of the ring finger of the left hand. The other fingers of the right hand rest outside the fingers of the left. The entire focus of the meditation should be "the *ch'i* and the heart/mind keeping mutual company in the *tan tien*." Professor also stressed that this style of sitting meditation was not necessary to our practice: "A lot of people seem to feel the need to be doing some sitting meditation, so for their sake, to keep them from going off in the wrong direction, I'm presenting this method."

I believe his hesitancy was because the idea of the *ch'i* in the *tan tien* could and should be practiced as often as possible in any and all circumstances: "riding a car or train, taking a walk, eating."

Tai Chi itself is meditation. "You should not sweat when doing the form or push hands," Professor said. "You don't sweat when you meditate so you shouldn't sweat when doing Tai Chi." (Sweating is an indication that the *ch'i* is dispersing.)

The meditation of Tai Chi is for the *ch'i*: when doing the form we should imagine the air to have the substantiality of water. The importance of this idea is reflected in the name often given to Tai Chi: "dry-land swimming." The more you feel the air like water, the stronger your *ch'i*.

The even, steady pace of the form — "like drawing silk from a cocoon" — moving as one piece, root and straight spine, all have the benefit of developing *ch'i*. Even relaxation itself, the basis of the study, is to remove all blockages, tension and hard force so that the passageways in the body are open to the flow of the *ch'i* and its accumulation.

34

The Tai Chi combat principle holds that "the battle is over when the swords cross." When two fighters make contact, the one who is softer will hear the intention of the other. On the advanced level that subtle, split-second understanding of intent is all that is needed for victory. So much of the endless, back-and-forth of push hands practice aims to develop the correct attitude, the ability to deal with the crucial first instant of contact. When grabbed do I resist in that first split second or do I instantly go with the opponent's intention? If I can go with his idea, he will go flying, but if at the first instant I resist even slightly it will already be too late.

You have to be completely relaxed, without any resistance. If you are 99% correct you are 100% wrong. This is why Tai Chi can be so frustrating: a practitioner can make a great deal of progress in subduing his ego but pay the price for a small residue of resistance in a split second of hardness that sabotages his best effort.

The principle is to be completely relaxed and receptive. "What is my opponent's intention?" I will relax and await the expression of his idea. It may be *yin* or *yang*, attack or retreat—that is all it can be though there are infinite variations on the theme. Whatever it is, I will follow. It is the nature of most martial situations that the opponent will initially attack rather than retreat. "Rollback" is the Tai Chi response to attack: give way before the attacker's force, turn to evade it, and simultaneously return the force to send him flying.

In push hands the basically receptive, nonaggressive quality of Tai Chi expresses itself in one's being able to deal with the opponent when he is in his strongest, most stable position.

"You must give him whatever he wants." Push hands is a metaphor for a fighting situation, and in a fighting situation you cannot expect the opponent to choose anything but his strongest position. Therefore to master Tai Chi, you must be able to play from the position that seems to be weaker, granting the forward, obviously substantial position to your opponent. If you can only gain victory from substantial positions you are depending on strength; you are not doing Tai Chi. Professor said that learning how to neutralize is ten times harder than learning how to push, but only if you can neutralize can you really do Tai Chi boxing.

To be able to neutralize and play off the back leg, you must have a root. To develop your root you must take pain. It's one of the reasons why Tai Chi is so good for your health, why there are 70- and 80-year-old Tai Chi masters who can demonstrate fantastic skill rather than sit in a chair and talk about it.

Ben Lo said of pain-taking that "you can take pain when you are young in order to be full of power when you are old, or neglect taking pain in your youth and have an old age full of pain."

Professor never liked to see his students sitting down in the middle of class. "You're studying *gung fu* here," he would say. "When I'm talking to you, you can still practice. Stand with your weight on one leg or the other. Never evenly distributed. With the weight predominantly on one leg, you are not double-weighted, which is stagnant, not alert. Also with the weight on one leg, you are working on your root." He encouraged us to maintain this attitude in all situations, not just class. Stand with weight on one leg, practice *gung fu*.

Even "investing in loss" has a supplementary benefit of developing the root. "Every time you relax and allow yourself to be pushed correctly, your root grows a little bit."

Professor was once asked, "When will my legs stop hurting?"

"When your legs stop hurting, you have stopped improving," was his answer.

35

What we play with in push hands is at the core of many of our relationship problems. During push hands class the following conversation is common:

First Student: "You're too hard, you're pushing on me like a freight train!"

Second Student: "Well, you're not soft, you're not yielding at all; you're like a brick wall!"

All push hands players have experienced this conflict. Its lesson is that if in pushing I find my partner straining in resistance, the fault also lies with my use of strength—if I were not being so insistent he could not resist me. Conversely, if I feel my partner's hard force building up on my body, it is because of my resistance—if there were no resistance, he would have nothing to push against. "It takes two to tango"; in push hands, a fight or life, conflict is based on an agreement between two parties.

Professor Cheng addresses this problem in his *Thirteen Treatises*: "When two people work a saw, their strength must be even so that there is no resistance in the forward and backward movement. If one side changes the balanced strength just a little, the teeth of the saw may get stuck. If the opponent lets the saw get stuck, I cannot keep going backward and release it by any amount of effort. I must first send it forward in order to resume the former motion.

"Give up oneself in order to follow others. When one can be in accord with the force, one can attain the wonder of neutralization.

"If the opponent moves only slightly, I shall have preceded the move. In other words, if the opponent uses force to press forward, I have already pulled back. If he has used force to pull back, I have preceded him sending my energy forward."

The hardness, egotism and willfulness underlying conflict also has health implications. In his commentary on Lao Tzu Professor said, "If one's will is too strong, it will not only harm one's primal energy but will also harm the very root and trunk of one's life span."

36

In ancient times in China, Professor told us, self-reliance meant that "a person could strap a sword across his back, and if he knew how to use it, there was no place he couldn't go."

The sword teaches how the application of Tai Chi principles extends to the use of an object, tool or weapon.

The sword is an extension of your hand and your *ch'i*. The arm must be completely relaxed so the *ch'i* can flow from the ground into the sword. Any tightness or tension in the arm and shoulder blocks the flow of the *ch'i* and forces you to manipulate the sword rather than allowing it to flow. Shifting the weight, turning the waist, allows gravity and centripetal force to move the sword. If the form is done properly, the player feels he is following the flow of the sword; the sword feels almost alive.

Fencing incorporates the same relational principles of listening and sticking that are present in the push hands exercise, but adds the dimension of moving the feet. Push hands uses fixed foot positions in order to exercise the waist. In the sword you move your feet to obtain positional advantage.

Rather than sticking to each other's hands, the players stick sword to sword, listening for the center through the sword. Just as in push hands, you neither resist nor insist but sense the opponent's force or resistance and flow around it to his center, the way water will flow around a boulder in a stream. As in push hands, you should not rely on disengagement or speed. Stick and respond to speed with speed, slowness with slowness. Your sensitivity allows you—in the words of the Sage of War, Sun Tzu—"to start after your opponent but arrive before he does."

The ability of a proficient Tai Chi swordsman to seem much quicker than his opponent is not a function of reflexes. Professor, in his 70s, could not have had the reflex speed of a younger opponent. He "got there first" because he heard the opponent's idea before the opponent was conscious of it, and his understanding of sticking gave him the advantage of his sword having to travel less distance than his opponent's. Sensitivity and its effect on the relationship of distance to speed is how an elderly person can overcome the speed of even a number of younger opponents.

Sensitivity also enables one to use leverage to "deflect a thousand pounds with four ounces" and be able to instantly return the opponent's force. In the case of the sword, the "return" is a counter-cut or thrust.

37

In the ten years Professor taught in New York, he took extended trips back to Taiwan on three occasions. His procedure in the weeks prior to a trip was to curtail his activities and rest, "like you allow a plant to rest when you are going to re-pot it."

A month before his second trip it was announced he would deliver a farewell address to the school in which, among other things, he would reveal his three secrets of life.

The school was jammed the afternoon of the address. Well over a hundred students were on hand to see him before he left and receive the treasures he had promised. Almost everyone had a notebook or tape recorder—the session was being videotaped as well. We could be assured that the three secrets of life would not escape our understanding.

The audience talked and fidgeted while the official video and tape recording technicians scurried about readying their equipment. Professor Cheng sat on a small platform facing the audience, quietly patient. Finally he began:

> Soon I am leaving to go back to Taiwan for a while.
> I am going to take the occasion of the end of the Tai Chi Chuan classes to say a few words.

The principles of Lao Tzu are the fundamental principles of Tai Chi Chuan. In Tai Chi you are taking the physical exercise, but the principle is in Lao Tzu.

Lao Tzu advocated the principles of *Tao* 2,500 years ago. The principles are based on the *Book of Change*, the oldest of the Chinese classics. There are three basic principles from the *I-Ching*:

The *Tao* of heaven. This means positive and negative, the two forces whose action and reaction govern everything.

The *Tao* of earth. All material things are governed by softness and hardness.

The *Tao* of man. The principles of benevolence and righteousness govern the behavior of human beings.

Of these three principles of *Tao*, Lao Tzu took the first and second to formulate his theory of the female overcoming the male, and softness overcoming hardness. Lao Tzu did not take the third principle of the *I-Ching*, the *Tao* of man. He did not believe in the *Tao* of man because he thought that men's actions are false. That is why he advocates Non-Action. But without the principles of benevolence and righteousness, how can we motivate the human race?

Human beings must talk about the *Tao* of man. Confucious, a contemporary of Lao Tzu, devoted his teaching to the *Tao* of man.

The difference between Lao Tzu and Confucius is that Lao Tzu emphasized long life and eternal vision while Confucius said, "If I can know the *Tao* of man, I can die the same evening without any regret."

I, Cheng Man-ch'ing, am of the opinion that the *Tao* of heaven, earth and man are three treasures. Since we are men, it is nothing if we just learn the *Tao* of heaven and earth. Understanding and behaving in accordance with the *Tao* of man will enable us to make a great contribution to ourselves, as well as to humanity.

Lao Tzu wants a simple society, where man can return to his primitive state. Confucius believes that as human beings we cannot escape the world, so we must learn to behave well in order to insure our happiness.

Lao Tzu wanted people to gain a long and healthy life. His principle was based on the breathing of the *ch'i*— nourishing the body by putting the *ch'i* into the *tan tien*. If you practice long enough you will gain the benefit of good health and long life.

To study the *Tao* of man by itself is no good. What is the good of having the *Tao* of man if you die? What is desirable is to have good health in order to carry out the *Tao* of man.

Study both sides of the coin—Confucius and Lao Tzu— in order to complete your knowledge.

The essence of Confucius' principle is based on "The Golden Mean": If I like something, you will like it too. If I don't like it, neither will you.

Now to change the subject. Since I am leaving, I want to repeat some words about the cultivation of the *ch'i*, so you won't forget.

When you become excited, your heart beats fast. When you swallow the *ch'i* into the *tan tien*, and have your feet planted firm on the ground, you will quiet down, your internal organs will be in harmony, and it's likely that your health will be good.

Besides cultivating the *ch'i* by directing the *ch'i* into the *tan tien*, there are some important secondary points I want to mention.

First, don't move too fast. Say that you are crossing the street and suddenly a fast car comes bearing down on you. You jump forward to get out of the way, but the car was swerving to avoid you, so you end up having jumped right into its path. If you had stayed slow, it would've had a chance to avoid you. So don't move too fast, and under all circumstances keep quiet and calm.

138

Also, don't be in too big a hurry to change your clothes with the change of seasons. Often you will see a day in winter where the temperature is suddenly warm, and many people will discard their winter clothes for a light shirt. But the *ch'i* of the earth is still cold, and it's very likely those people will catch a chill. The same is true of not changing your dress from warm to cold.

Don't eat too much. When you get hungry, don't gobble your food too fast or you will injure yourself. Eat slowly and always stop while you are still a little bit hungry.

There is one last point I want to discuss. In the past six years that I have been in New York, I have observed certain unsatisfactory conditions. Lao Tzu said to harmonize with light and be the same with the dust. There are a number who go against that principle, who want to act in their own way, who want to be different. It is best to harmonize with everyone else.

Also I hear so much talk about love. Confucius' concept of love had to do with husband and wife, man and woman — not *women*. If a man and woman find genuine love, they will stick together without change. Also, if you marry and don't produce children, you won't be following the *Tao* of heaven and earth.

Among my friends, there are some who treat love lightly. They play around for a while without any genuine love. If life is treated lightly — just playing around — after a time health will fail and life won't last long.

The talk ended on that note. As the audience milled around, the consensus seemed to be that this had been one of those periodic anti-climaxes that added spice to our experience of the old man.

I was very disappointed. Promised his "secrets of life" — it was obvious that he had discovered something transcendent — I

139

had received instead dry philosophy, plus the same familiar advice about conserving *ch'i* and other minor tidbits.

I saw where he was heading. That year he had delivered a series of lectures on Lao Tzu. After he returned from Taiwan, he would start lecturing on his real love, Confucius.

It seemed to me that on a certain level the old man was being dishonest. He had gotten his great power from Yang Cheng-fu, who was all but illiterate and, it was rumored, mysterious magical Taoists who certainly didn't deal in abstract philosophy.

Now in his old age he was turning cranky and moralistic, keeping his real secrets hidden while dunning us hippies with tired stuff about how we "shouldn't play around," that "marriage was for having children," and worst of all—to those of us who were in sympathy with the anti-Vietnam war movement, reaching its crescendo at that time—he was echoing the desperate pro-war establishment with his Confucian garbage about not acting in our own way, wanting to be different instead of harmonizing with society.

At that time even China had outlawed Confucius' teaching as being reactionary and outdated. "That must really stick in his craw," I thought.

When he returned from Taiwan, he gave two lecture series on Confucius' teaching, "The Doctrine of the Mean" and "The Great Learning." I took one, was bored silly and skipped the second, the only talks he gave that I missed in the time I studied with him.

Reflecting on this lecture 20 years later, I am once again impressed at how much smarter the old boy has gotten over the years. I am much more appreciative of Professor's directive to "harmonize" the teachings of Confucius and Lao Tzu and the principles that underlie them.

Spiritual growth cannot take place in a vacuum removed from the concerns of one's fellow human beings. How the specifics of Confucius' teaching hold up after 2,500 years is for me a moot point. The core of the teaching is timeless. The two central themes are *Jen* and *Yi*, generally translated as Benevolence and Righteousness. *Jen* is also translated as "Love," made up of the ideogram representing "man" combined with the ideogram representing "two." Two human beings. How do two human beings behave? Confucius said, "Don't do to another person what you would not have them do to you."

Benevolence does not stand alone. It is balanced with the idea of Righteousness. Professor said the character *Yi* means right and wrong. "Not," he said, "partly right or partly wrong. It's either one or the other." Justice.

Studying the *Tao* of man means exploring in thought and action *Jen* and *Yi*, Love and Justice. To love, to express love with the totality of one's being, is one of the secrets of life. It is the foundation for being with one's fellow man as well as for being with oneself. A problem arises when Love doesn't have Justice for balance. Love naturally extends to another— two human beings—my child, wife or friend, but what about people suffering in Central America? Benevolence needs the safeguard of right and wrong to counteract the limitation of being able to love one's own family, neighbors or country while ignoring, or perpetuating injustice on, the outsider who is a statistic or a subhuman.

The study of the *Tao* of heaven and earth and the study of the *Tao* of man require very different processes. Achieving the *Tao* of heaven and earth requires an essential unlearning— to let go of that which blocks the *ch'i:* physical tension, dictates of the ego and fearful conditioning. We have to "learn"

141

how to have faith in, and come to embrace, the crystalline child, the sage in our soul, who is already one with the *Tao* of heaven and earth.

The *Tao* of man is less transcendent and trickier because it involves the mind and ego, full of illusion, rather than the omniscient soul. The process involves gaining knowledge of the world.

Lao Tzu and Confucius were purported to have met, and Confucius' reaction was to admit that his teaching did not extend to Lao Tzu because "Lao Tzu is a dragon."

Relating the story of that meeting, Professor explained that in order to follow Lao Tzu's teaching, a person needed to live alone on a mountaintop. "To live in the world requires knowledge of the *Tao* of man."

Knowing right from wrong is not a birthright, though many spiritual seekers would argue this point. It is the height of ignorance, if not arrogance, to think we need only follow our heart to know justice in any particular social situation. What spiritual seekers generally consider to be the emanations of the heart—divine wisdom—is often a compendium of internalized propaganda, the conditioning of media, school and family, ingrained societal attitudes and prejudices. It takes study in depth, intellectual discipline and courage—not simply a pure heart—to separate truth from propaganda so as to balance Love and Justice in the world and in our lives.

The deepest challenge, in Professor's words, is "to harmonize the two teachings": to awaken the wisdom of the soul and combine it with the developed understanding of the mind, producing the warrior sages we need at this crisis in human history.

Wolfe Lowenthal was born in 1939 in Pittsburgh, and began his study of t'ai chi chuan in 1967 with Professor Cheng Man-ch'ing, in New York. Over the years he has worked as a typesetter, screenwriter and peace activist. He currently lives, studies and teaches at his school, the Long River T'ai Chi Circle in New York City.